This extraordinary story of how three people fought against appalling odds is one of the most moving and heartwarming ever to be told.
Leonard Wiles, an ex-lorry driver, badly wounded in the war, living in poverty but with a latent genius for engineering, marries Hazel.
Hazel is 20 years younger, married three times, born in a caravan, illiterate till the age of 18.
Leonard and Hazel discover Terry, an illegitimate, abandoned, severely physically handicapped little boy.
The story of this unlikely trio is the triumph of love, determination and skill over one of modern science's most tragic mistakes.

This is a true story; some minor names and relationships have been slightly altered.

Marjorie Wallace and
Michael Robson

On Giant's Shoulders

The Story of Terry Wiles

'A Dwarf on a Giant's shoulders sees further of the two.'
George Herbert (*Jacula Prudentum*)

CORGI BOOKS
A DIVISION OF TRANSWORLD PUBLISHERS LTD

ON GIANT'S SHOULDERS

A CORGI BOOK 0 552 10472 8

Originally published in Great Britain by
Times Books, the book publishing division
of Times Newspapers Limited

PRINTING HISTORY
Times Books edition published 1976
Corgi edition published 1977

Photographs by Peter Dunne

This book is set in Intertype 10 on 11 pt Lectura

Corgi Books are published by
Transworld Publishers Ltd,
Century House, 61–63 Uxbridge Road,
Ealing, London W5 5SA

Made and printed in Great Britain by
Cox & Wyman Ltd., London, Reading and Fakenham

A Road to Freedom

I would describe my life as a never-ending road with its bumps and smoothness. Sometimes I would be travelling on smoothly and then suddenly I would hit a bump of sadness in my life, but that bump would die away into nothing. Then I came to a hole when I thought life was not worth living. But as usual I carried on. Then suddenly I met two loving parents who ended my journey and who protected me from life's hardships. My father is a pioneer in his way because he invents machines to enable me and other physically handicapped children to lead a normal life.

Terry Wiles

To Doris Wallace and Judy Smithies
And to all children who suffer, and to
the parents who love and suffer too.
M.W., M.R.

CONTENTS

PREFACE

THE campaign for the victims of the thalidomide tragedy seems, recollected today, to have been a swift and certain affair. But memory plays us tricks. The *Sunday Times* took up the plight of the children and their parents in earnest in September 1972, it did not succeed until January 1973, and certainly in the first weeks we seemed to be making a dismayingly small impression on public, press, television and Parliament with the actuarial arguments about levels of compensation. Not until the High Court banned one of our articles in mid-November and the Commons had a debate at the end of the month did the campaign gain its own momentum. It was during this difficult period that we decided to feature each week the story of one thalidomide victim, a policy we could keep going, we reckoned in gloomier moments, for two years. There was one doubt, bred years ago when I first published stories of thalidomide babies: there had then been several complaints that it was not seemly somehow to focus on such events.

Nothing like that occurred when we began telling the stories of individual families in the autumn of 1972. The public responded at once with letters, and with cheques and messages. Marvellous encouragement it was for us, but especially for the families; and no story more dramatically caught the imagination than that of Terry Wiles, born without arms and legs, as a result of thalidomide. Any doubts about the 'difficult' nature of reading about deformity and deprivation was put to flight and to shame by this, the story of the lively Terry and his adoptive parents Leonard and Hazel. Marjorie Wallace wrote the outlines of it in the *Sunday Times*; in this fuller and more contemporaneous account she and Michael Robson have written an absorbing story and done justice to a remarkable family.

They have also provided enduring testimony of the idea that triumph may be born from tragedy.

HAROLD EVANS

HOW THE BOOK CAME TO BE WRITTEN

IT was a bleak, dank day in November 1972. My head ached and my eyes streamed with cold. Reluctantly, I forced my way through the rain to King's Cross to board a train for Huntingdon. As the train keened through the countryside and patches of fog slapped against the windows, I read through my notes:

WILES, Terrence (formerly Andy). Ten years old. Thalidomide. Dwarfed. Four-limb amelia. Complete absence of left eye; defective vision in the right eye. Likely to remain totally dependent on other people.

It was a familiar list of horrors. In the course of my work as a writer for the *Sunday Times*, I had to visit the homes of a hundred families who were no strangers to such deformities. These children, human shadows to what had become a major Press and Parliamentary campaign, were among the most pathetic sights I had ever seen in my ten years of journalism. There were nearly four hundred such victims scattered throughout Great Britain. Now reaching adolescence, they had been waiting all their lives for lawyers and executives to agree to compensate them, at least in money, for the imperfections wrought on them before they were born by a man-made drug. Terrence Wiles was on my list as one of the five most severely damaged children in the country.

Half-dreading the visit I arrived at the station. Leonard Wiles met me and drove the few miles to the cottage. We turned from the main road into a rough drive, littered with old farm implements and garden tools. Rattling over the pot-holes and watching the fog curdle ominously over the fields, I felt even more sorry that I had chosen this dismal day to come. At the end of the drive were two dilapidated cottages. Outside the door of the further cottage, an Alsatian barked.

We entered a small, cluttered room with no carpet, a lumpy settee and a few threadbare chairs. Hazel, Leonard's wife, poured us mugs of tea and the interview began.

An hour later, Leonard Wiles asked if I would mind accompanying him to the school to fetch Terry. At first, as the other children scrambled out of the classroom, Terry was nowhere to be seen.

'Ah! there you are, you rascal!' exclaimed Leonard. Not bargaining for the tiny size of the boy, I had failed to notice him on the floor at our feet. Leonard scooped up the wriggling, black-haired bundle and thrust it into my arms. It was an extraordinary sensation: there was nothing to catch hold of on this two-foot torso. I did not know whether to support his head like a baby or just cling on, hoping he would not slip through my hands. On the way home he sat on my knee and we began to talk. As a child, walking past the guillotine scenes in Madame Tussaud's, I had sometimes tried to imagine what it would be like if one of those fallen heads had begun to speak. Now I knew. But the first horror soon gave way to the greater necessity of keeping pace with an onslaught of intelligent questions: 'Where do you come from?' 'Which paper?' 'Ugh! Not that one!' 'What length of article?'

The hours went by. I missed one train after another. I had forgotten about the fog, my cold and my appointments in London.

The next day I returned to the office, bubbling over with the story I had found. My Features Editor was sceptical, but as I flooded his desk with more and more pages of notes, he too became involved. Three days later, on Sunday, 19th November, an article appeared.

The response was tremendous. There were letters and cheques for the family from all over the world.

During the next three years, I was drawn back again and

again to the cottage in the Huntingdon fields. Each visit was as stimulating as the first. I began to stay overnight and for weekends until I became part of the Wiles's lives.

Over lunch one day I explained my plans for a book to my friend and colleague Michael Robson. We spent a weekend with the Wiles and together we set out to fulfil my dream. That mission has now been completed.

For the Wiles family these years have brought the realization of many of their dreams. Terry is now a teenager and remarkably independent. But I shall never forget that first visit to the extraordinary trio and the first tea-time at Nursery Cottages.

The mugs had been cleared away and the sandwiches eaten.

'Tarumtara!' fanfared Terry, bouncing like a top-heavy jumping bean into my lap.

'Ladeez and Gentlemen. Allow me to commence!' Then, in vibrant voice, so loud it seemed impossible for it to come from so minute a source, he began to sing:

'If you're happy and you know it – clap your hands.
If you're happy and you know it – stamp your feet.'

And the tiny boy who could do none of these things, urged us on, conducting with his toes.

MARJORIE WALLACE

1976

PART ONE

Three Lives

CHAPTER ONE

THE DARK BACKWARD

EARLY-MORNING mist gave place to wintry sun, as the lorry forced its way southwards, through the tunnel, across the moonscape of north Kent, towards the gentler woods and heaths of Sussex. The driver leaned forward to wipe the film of condensation from the inside of the windscreen. His companion, a two-year-old Alsatian, shifted uneasily and attempted to lay her muzzle across the driver's knee. He lit a cigarette and glanced at his watch. He was much too early.

The driver, Leonard Wiles, was a broad-shouldered man in his middle fifties, with fair, thinning hair and a face that would seem at first to be more at home in the solitude of high fells than in the smoky interior of a lorry's cabin. A closer examination would reveal strange puckerings across the bridge of his nose, seamed flesh by his ears; and, running down his cheek, the striations and skin-hues that indicated facial surgery. The hands controlling the wheel were large and strong. Earth and oil lay embedded in the knuckles; the fingernails were short and chipped; the palms calloused. The man was dressed carelessly in a torn, oil-stained jacket, a green sweater frayed and running at the seams, and a faded khaki shirt. His trousers were baggy, the seat shiny with months spent in the driving-seat. The socks had been washed and worn too many times, and the shoes were cracked and split. Both soles were paper-thin. The driver's eyes, keen, hazel, moved constantly from the road ahead to a closer examination of the lanes that ran at right angles across ploughland and coppice west of his route.

His lorry contained shrubs and potted plants drawn from a

nursery at Brampton, in Huntingdonshire. Leonard Wiles had driven over a hundred miles since he had set out in the cold, grey dawn and he was now approaching his journey's end. The dog Sheba was delighted to stretch her legs and caper about as Leonard unloaded the nursery produce at a smallholding and briefly passed the time of day with one of his firm's customers.

Leonard looked at his watch. If he set off now he could be home for tea and the evening would be his. The lorry moved away north, gathered speed, and Sheba settled down again on her seat in the cabin. The village was three, four, five miles behind him, but there was no easing of the tension that was cramping Leonard's stomach. Perhaps unconsciously, his foot eased off the accelerator. The engine strained in top gear, and Leonard changed down; stopped the vehicle altogether. Sheba looked up at him, puzzled. This was not the routine she knew. She had had her run-around half an hour ago. Leonard reached for his map in the untidy, battered glove-compartment, reflected a moment, then unfolded it.

'Six miles,' he muttered. 'That's all it is.'

He finished his cigarette, and reversed the lorry into a side turning, then raced through the gears fast. Sheba sat up and peered out of the front window of the cabin as though she sensed his uncertainty.

Unemphatic countryside flickered past. Leonard saw that his right hand was shaking slightly. This is ridiculous, he thought, and angrily reached for another cigarette. He drove past a low complex of buildings and parked the lorry in a tree-enclosed, metalled area. Sheba looked at him hopefully.

'Better wait here,' he said.

He walked across to the nearest building and glanced about. No one was in sight. He opened the door and stepped into a wood-blocked corridor. Distantly a typewriter clattered; a pleasant smell of tobacco-smoke and flowers mingled with that of furniture polish. A woman's crisp footsteps rang on the floor, and Leonard paused uncertainly. The woman appeared, carrying a file of papers. She was startled by Leonard's presence and immobility.

'What is it? What do you want?'

'You have a child here called Andy,' he said. 'I'd like to see him.'

She looked at him doubtfully.

'Andy. I don't know whether it's convenient or not.'

'But it's Saturday, isn't it?' he urged. 'And I've come a long way.'

Her eyes travelled down his worn-out clothing, lingered on his cracked nails and crumpled, faded trousers. He could sense the doubt in her mind. Yet his voice, quiet and formal, seemed at odds with his appearance.

'I'll see if it's possible,' she said. 'You'd better come with me.'

Having made up her mind, the woman strode off briskly, and Leonard lumbered behind her, gripped again by irresolution and fear. His palms were sweating, and he wiped them on his thighs.

They were approaching another building now, and the woman called out:

'You've been here before, I take it?'

'No. Never.'

She stopped so abruptly that Leonard almost cannoned into her.

'You mean . . . you've never seen the boy?'

'No.'

'Then, forgive me, but why are you here? He's nearly six years old, and apparently you've shown no interest in him so far.' It was all becoming even worse than Leonard had feared.

'I was in the neighbourhood, you see, and I thought . . . I know the family. I've known about Andy since he was . . . born.'

The woman seemed at once impatient and compassionate. She glanced over her shoulder, then looked up at Leonard.

'I suppose you know what you're letting yourself in for?'

He nodded.

'I hope so,' she continued. 'They have enough to put up with as it is. I don't want you going in there unprepared.' This was a possible exit for Leonard: he was being handed it uncompromisingly. Instinctively he reached for his packet of cigarettes, then withdrew his hand as he realized the woman was waiting for his reply.

'I'd like to see him. Please.'

She nodded, turned, and reached the swing door. Leonard followed her inside uncertainly. Bleak sunlight clearly illuminated the room. Small faces looked up towards him. The woman was clicking swiftly towards one of the beds. Leonard walked slowly after her, trying not to look about him. He felt as if he were wading through a nightmare – one surpassing in naked horror all those he had experienced in the Middle East, when for weeks on end he had lain blind and bewildered in a field-hospital. But he had been a soldier then, and he and his fellow victims had been men-at-arms. But these were children! Leonard choked back the rush of bile to his throat. The woman was gathering up what appeared to be a baby in her arms.

'Mr. . . . er?'

'Wiles. Leonard Wiles.'

'Andy! There's a visitor here to see you, a Mr. Wiles.'

Giddy, aghast. Leonard attempted to force a smile to his mouth.

'Hello, youngster! How about getting dressed and coming out in my van?'

Leonard carried the five-year-old towards the lorry, where Sheba was sitting with her head out of the window, watching their approach.

'Coo, that's an Alsatian, isn't it? Bet he's fierce – is he a guard-dog?'

'He's a she, and she's called Sheba. She's supposed to guard the lorry, but she wouldn't hurt a fly. Come on, girl, this is Andy.'

Sheba began to nose at and lick the boy's feet.

'Doesn't half tickle. She won't bite, will she?'

Within minutes, Leonard's first reactions of disgust and pity had vanished. He realized he was in the presence of a lively, independent and strong-willed little boy, not the pathetic scrap of humanity he had first judged Andy to be. The child questioned him endlessly and intelligently about his job, his home, his wife; cadged sweets and enjoyed them as any small boy would do; and, when Leonard finally returned him to the ward, announced emphatically to his companions:

'My uncle's taken me out and he's got this big lorry and this great big Alsatian called Sheba and he's coming back again to take me out for a drive – aren't you, Uncle?'

The nurse now handling Andy said quietly, 'They always call visitors Auntie or Uncle.'

'I'll come back, Andy,' Leonard said. 'Bye now.'

'Goodbye. And thanks for the sweets.'

Leonard reached the door, and the remorseless little voice was raised again: 'Promise! You promise to come back!'

Leonard returned to the lorry, caressed Sheba a moment, started the engine, and began the 110-mile journey back to Brampton. He did not consciously change gear, slow down at tricky bends or halt at major roads ahead. His mind was fully occupied with the events of the morning.

During his war service Leonard had seen at first hand the full effects of mutilation on combatants: soldiers without limbs, some eyeless, some hideously burned. He had himself spent more than two years of his life in military hospitals. But he had never experienced anything to equal the shock and horror and helplessness that he had undergone when he first saw the children's ward – its occupants, and the tiny, black-haired, grotesquely deformed body of Andy. He drove home slowly, revolving in his mind what he could best say to his wife when he returned. Hazel was waiting for him at the cottage door – she had heard the lorry rumbling down the track that led to their home – and came to meet him as soon as he and Sheba had left the lorry.

'How did it go? What's he like?'

'Let's go inside, shall we, and have a cup of tea?'

The cottage was small, and their means minimal. Leonard and Hazel lived and slept in one downstairs room, their furniture a second-hand bed and two orange boxes. A small kitchen led off from the living-room.

'Well, Len, what do you think?'

Hazel – plump, dark-haired, bespectacled – was normally cheerful and full of the talk of the day when Leonard came home from work. Now, sensing his worry and confusion, she became subdued and anxious. Leonard's account of his visit to Andy in no way reassured her.

'I don't think I could face it, Len – I really don't. Not to see all those poor kids like that.'

Though still a young woman in her thirties, Hazel had undergone a number of major emotional crises, any one of which might have ended in total disaster for her. Life with Leonard had restored some of her confidence and pleasure in living. She was not anxious for the new, fine balance to be upset by a cripple she had never seen.

During the course of many conversations over the next few weeks she made her attitude clear to Leonard. He respected her hesitancy but urged her at least to accompany him the next time he had an opportunity to visit Andy.

'I'll have to think about it,' she told him. 'I've got to pluck up the courage to go down there, and it won't be easy.'

It took Hazel five months to summon up the courage, but one Sunday in March 1968, she and Leonard set off with Sheba to drive down to the hospital. When they arrived, they were told that Andy was in the day-room. Hazel gripped Leonard's arm.

'I'm so nervous, Len.'

But to her surprise and Leonard's relief, what she saw in the day-room was a six-year-old of normal height, wearing a normal jacket and long trousers.

'But Len . . .' she muttered.

'It's all right. He has his artificial limbs on.'

'Hello, Uncle,' called Andy, and tried to walk towards them. It took him several minutes to move a few yards. He stood swaying slightly, and looking up at them.

'Is this Auntie?'

'Yes, Andy. We've come to take you out for the day.' The child's face changed from wary enquiry to delight.

'Out of the grounds, you mean? Out of here?'

'Would you like that?'

'Smashing!'

Leonard checked with Sister Ford, who agreed that it would be an excellent idea if the boy were to get out and about for a few hours.

'But let's get him undressed and changed,' she said. 'He doesn't want his arms and legs on if he's out in the car with you.' The arms, harness, bucket seat and legs came off. Hazel could now see, for the first time, the extent of Andy's handicaps and his tiny size. Compassion fought with terror.

'Come on, love,' she said, and picked up the six-year-old as she might have swung a baby into her arms.

They drove into a town on the main road and asked Andy what he would like to do.

'Can we go to a café? I mean *inside* one, please? I've never been inside a café before!'

They found a large one and parked nearby. Sheba was left in the car, and Hazel, carrying Andy, walked towards the café, followed by Leonard. A number of people were clustered by the entrance, reading the menu and considering whether to go in or not. Conversation stopped as Hazel and Andy approached them. There were overt stares and the beginning of questioning whispers. Hazel stood irresolutely, flustered and embarrassed. Leonard joined her, and saw what was going on.

'We can't go through with this,' he muttered. 'This isn't a raree show. Come on, let's get him back to the car.'

'I thought we were going into the café,' protested Andy loudly. Hazel and Leonard paused again, and stared back at the curious faces of the watchers.

'Come on,' said Hazel, 'let's go, then!'

They walked past the starers and entered the café. At once Andy began to enthuse about the place, with its – to him – wide variety of goodies to eat and drink. But at the counter Leonard and Hazel paused again. Another thought had struck them simultaneously: how does an armless child eat and drink? Would they have to feed him?

'What's the matter?' Andy wanted to know.

'Tell us what we do now,' they implored.

'I'll show you,' he said.

He told Hazel what he would like: a salmon sandwich, a jam tart and a glass of orange juice. Hazel carried him to a vacant table, and Leonard followed with Andy's choice and their own.

'Put me in the chair, please,' said Andy. 'On my own.' They did so.

'Now would you put my food and drink on the edge of the table?'

They did so, and watched in fascination – as did the other customers in the café. Andy shuffled forward, took the rim of the glass of orange juice between his teeth, tilted the glass, and began to drink. Nothing was spilled. He set down the glass and prepared to eat the salmon sandwich. He drew it close to the edge of the plate with his chin, then took it between his teeth, bit cleanly, replaced what was left on the plate, and ate with evident enjoyment. After a few minutes, when it had become clear to everyone watching that Andy was capable of eating without assistance or mess, some of the curiosity waned, and the three of them could enjoy their snack without being continuously stared at.

The rest of the day passed without further strain. When they returned to the hospital, Leonard and Hazel were asked if they would like to have Andy home with them for the Whitsun holidays. They had not expected so frank an overture so early in their knowledge of the child, and demurred uncomfortably.

'We'd like to see him again, of course.' said Leonard. 'But for five days? Can we think about it, and let you know?'

'Certainly. But try to give us plenty of warning, will you? We like as many of them as possible to have homes to go to when there are public holidays. They become very bored here if they don't get away now and again.'

Hazel and Leonard were unhappy about what they considered to be this sudden emotional pressure.

'Yes, we'll let you know,' said Leonard.

Distantly, Andy was bellowing at them. Hazel and Leonard moved down the ward. The bright brown eye regarded them earnestly.

'I'm coming to the cottage, aren't I – at Whit? I can see all the places you've told me about!'

They walked across to the lorry.

'I can't, Len. I can't. It's impossible. What's the use of getting dragged into something when we know there's nothing we can do?'

'Give it time,' he urged. 'Just give it time.'

CHAPTER TWO

ANDY

ANDY was born on 12th January, 1962, at Thorpe Hall Maternity Unit, Peterborough. The doctors there did not think he would survive. He was brought into the world without arms, his shoulders neatly sewn over so that his little torso slipped through their hands as smoothly as the body of a new-born seal. He had no legs: instead two flippers, a cross between fingers and webbed feet, extended from either side of his trunk. A pad of muscle replaced his pelvis. One eye hung down his left cheek, pushed out of its socket by a sightless, white cyst. His nose was flattened so that it looked like a miniature saddle bridging the two sides of his distorted face.

The doctor and midwife had never witnessed the birth of so grotesque a creature before. They had seen pictures in textbooks of phocomelic children – those born with short arms or legs – but they had never imagined a baby with deformities as extensive as Andy's. Shocked and distressed, not daring to give voice to the thought that he should not live at all, they hurried into routine procedure and roused him into a cry of survival.

Curiously, it was when Andy was six years old and able to imagine the moment of his birth that he became fully aware of his body and its deformities.

'Auntie,' said Andy on one of his first visits to Nursery Cottages, as Hazel lifted him into bed, 'why don't children's doctors love children?'

'Of course they love children,' replied Hazel, 'otherwise they wouldn't help to bring them into the world.'

'If they love children why do they slap them when they are coming out of the hole?'

Hazel, wondering where all this was leading, gave him an explanation.

'I've got a good question,' persisted the little voice. 'How did they slap me then? I mean what could they hold on to to hang me upside-down?'

'When you came out,' Hazel continued hastily, 'I expect they just grabbed you by the ear and slapped you and that was how you came to life.'

Andy reflected a moment and seemed to accept her reply, and it was from that moment that he talked about his body and his lack of arms or legs.

From the start, Andy's expectations were grim.

The Furies that hummed around his birth spared none of their shafts. They heaped their curses on his head and tormented his small being with every possible affliction. Their destruction may have been complete but for one thing: whether through oversight or deliberately in the belief that it would only exacerbate the horrors of living with such a body, they left his mind intact. And, as the years went by, it was this lively, determined, sharp intelligence that prevailed, and outgrew his stunted limbs and ill-fated beginnings.

For even without his physical handicaps, Andy's birth was inauspicious. He was born to an unmarried girl from a poor family. His cinnamon brown skin and black curly hair suggested that he was also half-caste. The man who may have been his father disowned him, and his mother, lonely and frightened in her guilt, believing that he would not survive, left her disfigured baby at the maternity unit and did not return. Completely abandoned, Andy stayed seven months in the care of the nurses before being taken to the babies' ward at the Chailey Heritage Craft School and Hospital in Sussex. It was here that he spent the first nine years of his life.

Andy was one of the first of the sad troupe of limbless children to be admitted to the hospital in the wake of the production of the 'wonder drug', thalidomide. The drug, developed by the German firm, Chemie Gruenenthal, in the 1950s, was manufactured and sold under licence in Britain where it was available on prescription from April 1958 until its teratogenic (or 'monster-making') potential was discovered in 1961. It was withdrawn from sale in November of that year. It was called the 'wonder drug' because it was said to cure without the usual side-effects, headaches, pains, anxiety, sleeplessness, depression and even morning sickness, and it was especially this latter use that made the drug so popular with pregnant women. Realization of the damage to the unborn foetus by agents such as a virus like *Rubella*, the cause of German measles, or drugs which pass through the mother's blood stream into the placenta, had left doctors with few substances they dared prescribe during pregnancy. The manufacturers of thalidomide, Distillers Biochemicals Limited, however, had advertised it as completely safe during pregnancy. It was not until three and a half years after it went on the market that an epidemic of grossly damaged children was formally ascribed to the drug. By then over 5,000 children with dreadful deformities and, worst of all, incomplete brains, had been born in Germany. Similar tragedies were reported from Canada, Japan, Australia and all the thirty-five countries where the drug, under at least fifty-one brand names, had been marketed. In Britain there were over 400 victims with deformities ranging from a missing finger to complete lack of limbs. One of the cruellest features of thalidomide, however, was that it did not matter how many pills were swallowed. The most minute quantity, one or two white pills, smaller than aspirins, if taken at a critical time in the first weeks of pregnancy, could maim the foetus as viciously as large quantities taken over several months.

It is not known how many pills Andy's mother took. What is known is that she was prescribed thalidomide during her pregnancy and that Andy was born, one of the most misshapen casualties of a pharmaceutical mistake.

And that was how Chailey Heritage came to be Andy's first home. The school and hospital are scattered over several acres of rough heathland, not far from Sheffield Park, in rural Sussex. It is the home, either temporary or permanent, of 280 boys and girls with handicaps from spina bifida and cerebral palsy to missing arms and legs. The place, built in the Bourneville tradition of an ideal village founded on wealthy industry, came about through the bizarre Edwardian visions of Dame Grace Kimmins. She and a spinster friend, Miss Alice Rennie, both wealthy and eccentric ladies greatly taken by the fashionable artists of the day and the moral values of their craft revival movement, had the idea of establishing a school where crippled boys from the East End of London could taste sunlight and country air, and improve themselves by learning a useful craft.

Full of energy, Grace Kimmins found and bought an old Sussex farmhouse, which had been a workhouse, in which to start her school. She raised funds from her friends, including the Rolls family, whose younger son had joined forces with Henry Royce to build motor-cars. She arranged a take-over of another charity school in London and sold off its premises to raise more money. And she persuaded the most fashionable and eminent architect of the time, Norman Shaw, who had built New Scotland Yard, the Piccadilly Hotel, and the Gaiety Theatre in Aldwych, to design her new school, complete with Gothic-revival church, and tile-hung dormitories and schoolrooms.

The Guild of Brave Poor Things, as Dame Grace called her organization, selected these pale, skinny lads, their joints twisted with tuberculosis or rickets, and transported them to the remote Sussex heath where, in return for their keep and training, they were obliged to uphold the Dame's moral and religious ideals.

Some years later Dame Grace extended the Craft School to take in girls. She was fond of boys, but had little feeling for their crippled sisters, and her dislike of them, and her inflexible views on the mixing of the sexes, made her build a New Heritage for the girls to live in, a safe one and a half miles away from the main Heritage and the boys' wards.

The eccentric Dame went so far as to insist that two operating theatres, one for girls and one for boys, should be built for the pioneering orthopaedic surgery that was carried out at Chailey. Church services had to be held separately and at times sufficiently far apart to ensure that boys and girls did not pass each other in the grounds. Even the staff from the girls' dormitories at New Heritage were forbidden to go to the main school for fear of some contamination.

In spite of its unusual features, the Craft school flourished and, in response to the needs of casualties from the two world wars (Chailey accepted handicapped adults by then), expanded its medical side. By 1948 when the National Health Service was created, it was a fully-staffed hospital and became one of the first specialized hospitals to be incorporated into the new scheme.

By the time Andy arrived at Chailey, the well-meaning Dame was dead and the more eccentric practices swept away. The old buildings now became the school, and the New Heritage the home and hospital for both boys and girls. New buildings had been added, although still in the same village craft tradition. Andy's first home was the Princess Elizabeth ward, an imposing loggia of stone columns and french windows curving gently round a sunken garden. From the back it was less imposing, and revealed its true construction as a curved wooden chalet. But it was warm and sunny and a pleasant enough place for babies and toddlers to grow up, as yet unaware of the handicaps they had.

At five Andy moved across the green to his new home. Tidemills ward was brightly painted like the rest of the hospital and strewn with posters and toys. Between eighteen and twenty children slept in the dormitory which adjoined a large day- and school-room. As it was on the first floor, a gentle ramp let the wheel-chair children propel themselves to the garden below. But despite its paint and sunny outlook it was, unmistakably, an institution where children had to be treated in numbers and where there could be little scope for individual waywardness. To Andy, with his beanstalking imagination. those bright walls were the bars of his prison. He had never experienced a house or any way of life outside the hospital, but he knew something better must exist and he was determined to find it. After six o'clock, which was the official bedtime, he would while away the evening hours plotting his escape. As the shadows stretched over the ceiling and cups chinked as the night nurse settled down to her tea, Andy, with the latest television serials still flickering through his mind, would conjure up his schemes.

He was the Great Escaper. He was Houdini breaking out of a sealed coffin. He was a prisoner of war, dodging bullets as he slid from knot to knot of torn sheet down the slippery walls of the castle. He was Andy the Invincible, Leader of the Resistance, planting explosives into the tops of German jackboots while his men escaped through the smouldering bars of their torture chamber.

'Quick! Run! Over the back wall and into the woods!' he would whisper breathlessly to his sleeping companions.

'Jacques is waiting. He will take you to safety. If there is any trouble, shoot!'

'Now,' he muttered to himself, 'You German blackguards, take this!' He hurled his incendiary across the ward so that it landed in Sister Ford's tea cup. He burst out laughing.

'Andy, what do you think you are doing?' came the expected voice, only this time it was thick with German gutturals.

'Nothing, Herr Ford,' he replied cheerfully as he dodged the approaching shadow and sprinted across the room to position himself for a second aim. This time he intended to blow up the whole building.

'Andy! Get back under the cover and take that marble out of your mouth.'

Andy, subdued, wriggled under the cover and let the marble fall to the floor. He felt the sheet with his tiny flippers and wondered whether he would ever be able to tear it up and tie it into knots. He would let himself down that wall – he had spent hours marking off in his mind where the cracks were – and then drop, ever so quietly, on to the grass. He would roll away across the road, into the forest, away from Chailey and the doctors and nurses, away from the white room where they stuck needles into his neck, away from the school where he was trapped for so many hours in the slow-moving prison of his artificial legs. Out there he had friends who would help him. There was always Trixie. She was gentle and loving. Anyway she owed him a favour. He had once saved her life. . . .

It was after tea in the ward. The late afternoon sunlight spun through the windows, edging with gold the white glare from the television set. Andy sat propped against the spokes of a wheelchair watching one of his favourite programmes. The other children, their damaged bodies no longer hidden in the chain-mail of harnesses and limbs, stretched their short legs on the floor or rested a half-grown arm on another's shoulder. The sunlight burned on a pile of iron calipers and metal braces taken off for the night and left in a corner. It was a pitiful sight, twenty children between the ages of five and nine, with stunted bodies and missing limbs, relaxing in their night clothes after a day's school. Andy looked around the faces of his fellows. His interest in the programme gave way to a desperate desire to take flight. He shuffled up to a group of boys sitting on the floor and confided his plans for escape.

'Can you keep a secret?' he asked.

They nodded.

'I'm going to escape. Only for a little while. I'll be back at the end of the next programme. I just want to plan a route so we know our way in the dark when we do it properly. Do you want to come?' His friends agreed to help him but they didn't want to miss the programme.

'We're scared.'

Andy made his plans. First, he would go to the dormitory, search the cupboard where they kept his cut-down pyjamas, and lay them out ready to change into when he returned, covered in dirt and twigs. Then, he would get himself past the ward, into the corridor, out on the ramp and away.

He was soon rolling down the grass slopes on to the road that separated the Heritage from the woods. A car drove past, not noticing the bouncing ball with glasses and a shock of hair. It spattered him with mud. 'Never mind,' he thought, 'that makes my camouflage better.' He rubbed his face and glasses as best he could against a piece of turf and continued over the road and into the forest.

The pine trees stretched miles above him. Evening mist curled around their dark trunks so that they seemed to wade around him like giant fishermen, their wellingtons washed white with foam. Andy was afraid. Then he heard a cry for help through the great rustling of the trees. He followed the whimpering sound until he came to a clearing. There, caught in a hunter's trap, was a beautiful fox cub with a delicate nose and anxious eyes. Andy laid his cheek against her fur and soothed her.

'Don't cry. What's your name? I'll call you Trixie – that's a good name for a fox. Now stay still and I'll lift off this spring and you'll be free. If you wait here tomorrow, I'll even bring you some of my dinner.'

Andy gently lifted off the spring and let Trixie bound back among the trees. She would wait for him tomorrow, he was sure of that and the next day and the day after.

'Andy! Where have you been?' scolded the nurse, lifting him in her arms. 'You'll catch your death sitting out on the ramp. All the others are in bed.'

Andy smiled to himself. He was not going to stay in that hard bed all his life. Out in the forest, he had a friend. She would help to set him free.

His bed in Tidemills dormitory was high and had bars on either side to prevent the restless little boy from falling out. At first Andy was allowed to sleep in a low bed from which he could drop down on to the floor. But his nocturnal wanderings tired the nurses who were always picking him up from the corridor or day-room or from under their feet. In the high bed, he could never reach the floor. He could no longer go searching for books or sweets he had hidden away or beg the nurse for a glass of water. If he couldn't sleep, it was just too bad. He would have to lie awake and stare at the ceiling. . . .

As he grew older and found his fantasies less comforting, Andy began to feel more and more convinced that he was being punished. Somewhere he had done something wrong and that was why God had taken away his arms and legs. Chailey was a place to which naughty children were sent when their mothers didn't want them any more. That was why no one loved him except perhaps the lady caretaker who would give him a quick peck on her rounds through the wards. At these times Andy hated everyone, especially children who had arms and legs. They were the arch-enemy. They were odd, monstrous creatures who had no human feelings. They were not made the same way as him and his ward mates. They did not even laugh or cry at the same things. They were callous and aloof. Andy could not remember being friendly with a normal child when he was at Chailey. Years later he recalled his feelings towards them: 'You see, we hadn't been told that they were just like us, that they had brains – well, some of us had brains – and they could talk, see and hear like us. We didn't know that then. The sisters never taught us to understand people with arms and legs.'

But almost as hostile as the gap between the normal and handicapped was the warfare that would break out from time to time between groups of damaged children within the wards. Those lucky enough to have arms to propel wheel-chairs would gang up on the short-limbed or limbless ones who had to shuffle on the floor. Sometimes they would line up their wheel-chairs like an army and charge the more vulnerable victims. Then, interlocking their wheels, they would form a circle to trap the luckless one who did not get away. But they did not always have the easy victory they would have liked to claim. The floor-bound children had the advantage of speed and size. They would scuttle away under the beds to fetch ammunition. Marbles would be placed under the wheels to make them skid. The more daring would creep up behind the enemy wheel-chairs and try to puncture their tyres with nails or broken tins. Then spare calipers would be bandied about as useful but dangerous weapons. One swing from a metal leg could send the floor-bound children flying in all directions.

Once strapped into their artificial arms and legs, however, the children like Andy were completely at the mercy of the less handicapped. They could only stand or move slowly away a few inches at a time. A knock, especially for a child without arms to protect his fall, could be serious and once on the ground there was no way he could flex the unbending tangle of metal to get himself upright again. He was as helpless as an upturned fly.

In 1960–61, when the first thalidomide children came to Chailey, doctors had little experience of dealing with such complex and terrible deformities. They tried to compensate for lack of arms or legs by strapping artificial limbs to the little bodies. But artificial limbs, difficult enough for an amputee, are even more unwieldy for children whose limbs have never been formed and who have only limited muscles available to operate them. Dr. Philip Quibell, the doctor in charge at Chailey, heard that engineers were developing power-operated arms for some German thalidomide victims. He sent to Germany and tried them out but they were awkward to wear and crude in their movements. The engineers tried again. The Aldermaston laboratory, which had produced the British atomic bomb, became interested. Everyone was trying to apply the most sophisticated engineering of the space age to make substitute arms for the handicapped child.

The results were ingenious, mechanically sound but otherwise grotesque pieces of apparatus, driven by gas compressed in a cylinder. The children hissed and creaked as they practised the control of this portable pneumatic crane attached to their body, pushing valves with their chin or pulling their shoulder in a vain attempt to lift food neatly from their plates to their mouths. All along, it seemed, the human problems were forgotten in the technical designs; the engineers tended to overlook the fact that what was a mechanical delight to them could be agony for the child who had to live with it. One engineer, when asked how the children felt in the bucket harness of their artificial legs – did they feel as if they were sitting or standing? – expressed surprise. 'That's an interesting question,' he said. 'I've never thought to ask them.'

When Andy was young they were experimenting with artificial arms attached to a jacket filled with plastic. It was not only heavy, it was hot. Someone had forgotten that children are active creatures who generate heat and sweat until one child was found to be running a temperature of 106°F, poached alive in his jacket and arms. Many such difficulties have been overcome but the dedication of the doctors and engineers could never compensate for the fundamental problem; that children wearing artificial arms could be no more than crane drivers, unable to feel or touch the objects they moved.

The legs, aluminium pylons which extended from leather saddles, were also cumbersome and unattractive. Their main advantage was that they could be adjusted to grow with the child so that he was the right height for his age and they averted the dismay of outsiders unused to thaolidomide damage. Today there is less emphasis placed on the wearing of limbs. Over the years their effectiveness, except for cosmetic reasons and particular activities, has proved questionable, and many of the thalidomide children now in their teens have discarded them altogether. Andy, however, was treated in the days when artificial limbs were fashionable. He never got used to his attachments. Although he had been fitted with arms and legs and encouraged to wear them from the age of eighteen months, he could never accept their weight and discomfort. The brace around his chest supporting his arms cut into his skin or rubbed against it, making him hot and itchy. The split hooks at the ends of the machine extensions were clumsy and inaccurate. He could feel nothing through the metal and preferred to scoop up the food with his mouth and chin rather than trust to the robot's haphazard thrust. His legs were even more uncomfortable. Each morning he was woken up and strapped into the bucket saddle which supported two aluminium pylons which he could pivot a few inches forward by rolling first to one side then the other. It would take him about ten minutes to swing his unsteady way from one end of the ward to the other, and once he got there all he could do was to stand precariously, or walk awkwardly back. His flippers, with which he could learn to do so much, were trapped in between the pylons and hidden under long trousers.

Breakfast was taken standing up. Once in his armour Andy could never sit down or shift his position except to wriggle his buttocks inside the saddle. He even looked forward to potty time because this meant a respite from the legs, although in every other way it was an unsavoury hour – twenty handicapped childen all lined up on their pots, some overbalancing, spreading the mess over the floor, others trying to jump from one pot to another to sit next to their special friend, while a nurse rushed back and forward to coax and clean them all.

After breakfast and potting his legs were strapped on again and the day's lessons began. Those children who, like Andy, had to wear artificial legs took all their lessons 'standing up'. They worked at high tables with a semi-circle cut out of the side facing them and a locking back to hold them safely trapped in the wooden bay. They would watch with understandable envy the children who had enough of their own limbs to be able to sit at low desks. As the hours of the lessons dragged by, they would still be standing, a phalanx of little tin soldiers wearily clinking from one metal leg to the other. Lunch was also eaten standing up. This was followed by an afternoon rest and a welcome removal of the limbs. Then the afternoon schooling or training session began, accompanied by the ache of more hours of standing and balancing on their metal stalks.

'I look like Frankenstein's monster,' said Andy with a grin, but he dreamed all day of the moment when he would be unshackled and could roll freely about the floor again.

The weekends were Andy's only pleasant memories of his hospital home. On Saturday and Sunday they did not have to wear their limbs and were left to their own devices. On Saturday television was left on in the ward and they would play games of ball or chase. Parties would occur spontaneously and the day-room was turned upside down. Some weekends a minibus would take them on an outing to a fair or the Zoo.

Sundays could be quite fun, too. In the morning they would all go across to their own church in the Old Heritage. Student volunteers would gather together all those who could not walk and push them in a hay wain across the heath. After church, the Tuck Shop Trolley was wheeled from ward to ward, and with all the buying and swopping, Tidemills resounded like an Eastern bazaar. In the afternoon parents and visitors would arrive. Andy did not have any parents and he was used to amusing himself when his friends were taken out to tea or when they went home during the long summer holidays. There was always a small group of children whose families could not have them at home or did not want them, who would be left behind. But Andy did have Elizabeth. On some Sundays and for several weekends this kind lady, captivated by Andy, visited him and took him to her home. It was the first time Andy had seen a house and he was impressed. She spoiled him with sweets, ice-creams and toys, and it was through her that he caught his first glimpse of a world outside. After a while, however, she felt unable to manage the aggressive and coercive little boy, and wrote a letter to his guardian asking if her visits could gradually cease.

He had other visitors, strangers who would volunteer to take him on the common or to the swings. They always promised to come back next week. But they never came. Andy learned early in life that promises were made not to be kept, that grown-ups may mean well but were afraid to get involved, and that in order to get anything you had to scheme and demand.

He was lying in wait, planning to fasten his tiny shell and flippers to anyone who stayed long enough in his life for him to get a hold. He wanted a family and a house of his own. He didn't know exactly what they meant, but his instincts drove him, like an animal in search of an essential food, towards them. Bitter, continually disappointed, his childhood fantasies rapidly drying up into wastes of self-pity, Andy let himself be looked after like a baby. If he wanted anything, he shouted; if he dropped a book or a toy, he would demand that it should be picked up immediately. He had been punished for a crime he could not remember committing and he had no qualms about punishing the world in return.

Andy was sitting on the covers of his bed waiting for a nurse to pick him up after his afternoon rest. It was a cold November Saturday and his little body, clothed only in underpants, shivered. It seemed he had been there for hours: the nurse was late this afternoon or she had forgotten him. He turned towards the window behind the bed and looked out at the black branches of the trees quarrelling with the fog and low sky. That meant they would not go out today and he would have to stay in the ward. Tears ran down his face but, lacking hands to brush them away easily, he did not make the extra effort of falling on to the pillow to rub his face. Anyway he would not be able to sit up again. He heard a nurse call his name, but he did not look round.

'Andy! There's a visitor here to see you, a Mr. Wiles.'

He turned and looked up. Above his bed towered an oldish man with a wide, craggy face and wispy hair. His clothes smelt of the road and his hands were stained with earth and oil. He smiled at Andy and his eyes looked kind.

'Hello, youngster! How about getting dressed and coming out in my van?'

CHAPTER THREE

LEONARD

HUNTINGDON in 1912 was a small, quiet market town lying among some of the most fertile acres in England. It had charm and some independence of spirit: was it not Huntingdon that had reared the only man ever to interrupt the English monarchical system – Oliver Cromwell? Its inhabitants, perhaps five thousand of them, knew their own businesses very well indeed and not a little about their neighbours' business too. And by any standards Charles Wiles was a man to raise your hat to – a lay preacher at the Methodist chapel, confirmed non-smoker, devout teetotaller and, most telling of all, proprietor and manager of two thriving confectionery shops. If there was one trait that marked Charles Wiles as a man slightly apart from his fellow-tradesmen in the Chamber of Commerce it was his passion for the internal combustion engine: a lay preacher on a motor-bike?

Charles Wiles and his wife, Betsy, contributed generously enough to the population of Huntingdon. Leonard was the fifth of six children to feel the benefit of confectionery affluence in the serene years immediately preceding the First World War. Leonard's childhood was peaceful, ordered and happy. Charles Wiles took his Methodism seriously, but he was not given to laying down the ecclesiastical laws except on the Sabbath, which he and his family observed with scrupulous care. Leonard, his three sisters and two brothers were given freedom to develop according to their individual tastes and requirements. For them, the greatest excitement was a local fire. Two dray-horses from the George Hotel would be hurried from their stables in the mews and down to the fire station, where they would be harnessed to the fire engine itself. Then the entire equipage would jolt and clatter down the High Street in search of flames, followed and in many cases preceded by an unruly mob of children offering advice, instruction and encouragement.

At first the World War had little, if any, effect upon the inhabitants of Huntingdon. They did not appreciate the nature of the conflict until red-faced farmers' boys marched off in innocence to Flanders, and failed to return. By the time Leonard was old enough to understand the meaning of war, the local Sunday School had been commandeered by the military as a temporary base for German prisoners of war. From there they would set off each day to work on local farms, their iron-shod boots clanking over the granite blocks of the main square. One of these prisoners Leonard was to remember with affection and gratitude a few months later: a tall, venerable man with a long grey beard, whom Leonard and his friends named 'Grandad'.

At an early age Leonard weighed the advantages of schooling and truancy, and found education wanting. One afternoon he made his way to a massive meadow, where he could see the prisoners of war gradually clearing the river of reeds and dead vegetation. Having assured himself of a lonely stretch of water Leonard settled down to fish, with his length of cane and a bent pin. An hour went by, and Leonard had caught nothing. Then he felt a hand on his shoulder. Startled, he looked round and up into the sober, bearded face of the prisoner Grandad. Without conversation, but with infinite care, Grandad instructed Leonard in the art of coarse fishing. It was a lesson that Leonard absorbed with reverence, and an afternoon that was to assume considerable significance much later in his life. It was without doubt the first time he had ever regarded a German as anything other than 'one of them Jerry soldiers'.

On Armistice Night Huntingdon celebrated as vivaciously as any country town in England. There were speeches, bonfires, dancing, drinking and endless carillons from the local churches. And there was – inscrutably and senselessly – a parade of the German prisoners of war through the victory-drunk streets. Leonard stood on a barrel, eagerly looking for his friend

Grandad, waiting to wave goodbye. But the occasion went dreadfully wrong. Someone threw an apple at a prisoner; someone else threw pieces of kindling. Within seconds the prisoners were being pelted with anything that lay to hand, and Leonard's last impression of Grandad was the old man's refusal to defend himself against the missiles as he marched stoically through the rabble, while his companions covered their heads and faces. Leonard went home and sobbed.

The following year, Charles Wiles renounced motor-bikes and bought his first car, a single-cylinder Sunbeam with chain-drive. Leonard was awed, impressed, and insatiably fascinated with what went on under the bonnet. It was a second-hand vehicle and notoriously temperamental, but Charles and Leonard seemed to derive as much enjoyment from tinkering with it, improvising spare parts and jury rigs, as they did from the family outings.

In 1921, while Leonard was still at elementary school, the family experienced two wholly unexpected disasters: Charles Wiles and Leonard's brother, Donald, died within months of each other. Leonard became more of a solitary child. He had little in common with his elder brother Albert, and even less with his sisters. Leonard fished as long as the weather would permit it, and when the streams and ponds rang with ice, he made himself a pair of skates. So absorbing did these spare time activities become that Leonard spent more and more time away from school. In the elementary school this was just about feasible, and no one appeared to care greatly. But when Leonard entered the local grammar school he found that playing hookey was not tolerated. At first Leonard made a token attempt to come to terms with the academic life – if only for his mother's sake. In his first year he achieved First Prize for general competence in his studies, and was regarded as a promising pupil. He had a quick mind, but one that was easily bored. When he saw no practical bearing in a subject he tired of it, and soon his reports became catalogues of academic delinquency. His master believed in giving value for money: if Leonard was recalcitrant, they were not to be ignored. By the time he was thirteen he had at least mastered the arts of speaking and writing both fluently and cogently. He chose to neglect everything else. Inevitably, Leonard was summoned before the Headmaster and told to give an account of his shortcomings. The boy pointed out his impatience with schoolwork and his very real concern that his mother could not physically handle the amount of work that two thriving businesses demanded. The Headmaster had words with Mrs. Wiles, with Leonard's masters, and with the local Education Officer. Eventually, Leonard was released from school at thirteen and a half, and went to work full-time for his mother.

It was more full-time than even Leonard had expected. From Monday to Friday he would work in the shop from eight in the morning until nine at night. On Saturday, the gala day, he seldom finished before ten or half past ten at night. In those days, where a family business was concerned, there was no statutory limit to the number of hours a child might put in, and as Leonard advanced into adolescence and early manhood the hours grew longer. He discovered within himself a massive patience for work whose value he acknowledged and understood, for work which directly benefited his family.

Such spare time as he had in the hours between working and sleeping was bound to occur late at night, long after friends had sought the customary amusements of the period. So Leonard had to choose occupations that befitted the solitary. He had clearly inherited from his father a knack with machinery of any sort. When he was scarcely nine years old he had observed that his mother's first new car, a bull-nosed Morris, was giving trouble. At half past six one morning, whilst preparing breakfast, Betsy Wiles noticed that Leonard was suspiciously absent from the kitchen. She went out into the yard and heard mechanical noises coming from the stables-turned-garage. She hurried into the garage and found an oily Leonard squatting by the entire contents of the engine.

'What on earth do you think you're doing, child?' she asked, not unexpectedly.

'I've taken it to pieces,' he pointed out. 'It's the only way to find out what's wrong with it.'

'But you'll never be able to put it together again properly!'

'Oh, yes, I shall,' he said confidently. 'You see, I have a scheme. As I take each part out I lay it down in order. When

I've found the trouble and fixed it, I shall put all the parts back, just as I took them out. Don't worry, honestly.'

Betsy stood a few moments, undecided whether to laugh or to box his ears. Eventually she went back to the kitchen. Leonard did not appear for his bacon and eggs. The other children washed up. Still no sign of Leonard. It was time to open up the shops. Reluctantly, Betsy returned to the garage. The bull-nosed Morris, bonnet down, stood throbbing quietly in the corner, and Leonard was washing his hands and arms at the pump.

'But – it's going! It's all right!' said Betsy incredulously.

Leonard nodded solemnly. 'Just needed de-coking, that's all.'

There was a limit to the number of cars available for Leonard to tinker with, and in the early twenties, when radio was in its infancy, Leonard discovered a new outlet for his creative talents. He progressed rapidly from crystal sets to more advanced models, and at one time the Wiles household boasted no fewer than five radio sets. The family's custom of regular visits to the movies continued, through spasmodically now, and when the movies became the talkies Leonard developed a new enthusiasm. He had hitherto been able, with a projector of his own devising, to entertain family and friends with films borrowed from local cinema managers. But the moment Jolson sang *Sonny Boy*, Leonard realized that sound-on-film was inevitable, and he reckoned with it on his own terms. From first principles he constructed a projector capable of conveying sound-on-film, and he kept his device a secret. Late one Saturday night he slipped out of the house and paid a visit to the projectionist at the Huntingdon Cinema. At that time every projection-room carried a number of stand-by films, dated B-reelers that could be shown if the main attraction caught fire, or was not delivered on time.

'I want a stand-by,' said Leonard. 'The biggest, brashest, noisiest standby you have.'

'What about a Western?' suggested the projectionist.

'Plenty of action?'

'Full of it!'

'And music?'

'The music's marvellous!'

A tin of mint humbugs changed hands, and Leonard darted

back to the parlour on the first floor with a can of film. He laced it through his new projector, checked his newly built, massive amplifiers, then swaggered down to the kitchen.

'Come on, everyone! The show's about to begin.'

His mother, brother and sisters, kith, kin and friends, squeezed upstairs into the parlour overlooking the High Street. The windows were flung wide open.

'Necessary,' said Leonard, solemnly. 'Fire hazard.' It was about midnight when Leonard Wiles, confectioner and impresario, presented *Idaho Riders* to an audience of nine and to most of Huntingdon – by virtue of the open windows. A crowd collected on the pavement outside and below, neighbours telephoned the police, doors were banged, walls thumped . . . but Leonard knew his twenty minutes of glory.

When Neville Chamberlain announced that Britain was at war with Germany, Leonard was twenty-six, and business-oriented. The Royal Air Force was establishing aerodromes throughout the flatlands of East Anglia, and two, at Witham and Nutwood, were within striking distance of Huntingdon. The NAAFI invited tenders for the supply of vegetables. Leonard bought a large field, at that time planted with young spring cabbage, and tendered. His quotation was accepted, and Leonard took to visiting his new possession with mounting excitement.

By the early summer of 1940 the field looked promising. Leonard began assessing the number of cabbages he could confidently expect, and the profit he confidently hoped to make. But one night Hermann Goering sent in the Luftwaffe to shake up the East Anglian aerodromes, and the following morning when Leonard cycled across to his field, he found that high explosive bombs had totally destroyed his hopes. Two massive craters and a quantity of shredded vegetation lay before him. Leonard actually shook his fist at the innocent sky: 'Oh, you bastards!' he declaimed. 'You rotten bastards!'

That afternoon, Local Defence Volunteer Wiles, L., presented himself for full-time combatant service with His Majesty's Armed Forces.

After the normal period of recruit training, during which Leonard thought seriously of deserting, so pointless and unrelated to the war effort did it seem, he was posted to Shoeburyness with the Royal Artillery. One day, volunteers knowing something about radio were commanded to step forward. Leonard sprang out, gave his name, rank and number, and was told to step back into ranks. A fortnight went by, and Leonard had forgotten the incident completely, when there advanced on Leonard's squad a young subaltern, asking for Gunner Wiles. Leonard was taken to the Battery Office and interviewed by a plump, genial major.

'Right, Wiles – you'll do. We'll be sending for you.'

'What's it all about, sir?'

'Hush-hush, Wiles. Top secret. Finger to your lips, Wiles.'

'Sir.'

'All right, Wiles. Off with you.'

Eventually Leonard found himself at St. Audrey's School for Girls in Westcliff-on Sea, at a radar school, utterly, and for the first time in his Artillery career, at home.

Leonard's years of improvisation were now paying dividends. His instructor soon realized that Leonard was way ahead of his colleagues in the radar class, and soon Gunner Wiles was being seconded to anti-aircraft units, to service or repair radar sets. It was during one of these visits that he met Robert Watson-Watt, the pioneer of radar, and, in Leonard's words. 'the most confidence-provoking chap I ever met during the war. After half an hour's conversation with Watson-Watt I realized that we could, quite probably, win the war in the air.'

Leonard did so well in the qualifying examinations that he was recommended to apply for entry to a Radar Instructors' course; but the plump, genial major had no intentions of losing a handyman such as Gunner Wiles. So instead of going down to Watchet for the start of the course, Leonard found himself embarking for Bombay, and the sharp end of the war.

Leonard served in the short, bizarre campaign in Iraq, then was posted to Egypt, where he contracted dysentery. He awoke in great pain to find that, by some weird War Office error, he had been sent to a hospital for soldiers mentally disabled by the rigours of the desert war. He was eventually released from there, convalesced, and hitch-hiked his way to Tobruk, where he caught up with his own radar unit.

After Alamein, Leonard was part of a convoy driving by night, and without lights, in a secret rush to establish a forward base. Leonard, by now a corporal, was sitting in the cabin with the driver, peering at the gloom of the desert ahead, when a tank-transporter, also without lights, collided with Leonard's vehicle. A tank of petrol caught fire, Leonard's vehicle lurched, and a driving mirror exploded into Leonard's face, splintering him with broken glass. After separating the vehicles, Leonard collapsed, stunned and temporarily blind.

He was sent to an R.A.F. field hospital where, fragment by fragment, the glass was removed from his eyes. Recovery meant further desert warfare, then preparation for the invasion of Sicily. And it was here that Leonard's army career came senselessly, ingloriously, to an end.

Following the establishment of Allied Forces in Sicily, a number of units were given twelve hours' local leave. Leonard, now an established two-striper, took a lorry-load of troops into the town of Catania, and the town was painted the appropriate colour in a short space of time. Leonard, who had enjoyed his break in a tavern, reported back to the town square, where the troops were mustering for their return. A sergeant approached Leonard and begged a lift back. Leonard, jovial with alcohol, pointed out that if the sergeant did come back, he would be in charge, as he outranked Leonard. The sergeant, possibly a shade less drunk than Leonard, agreed, called the nominal roll, and climbed up in the cabin of the lorry with the driver. Leonard went into the rear of the lorry with the gunners.

Night, a light rain, a wary driver and a somnolent sergeant beside him. The lorry eased forward, slit headlights scarcely picking out the physical features of the journey. Italian railwayman, vaguely visible waving a red light, shouting something in his native tongue. Blearily, the lorry driver braked, and lowered his cabin window.

'What you on about, Jack?'

A vigorous reply in Italian. The railwayman was understandably anxious – the lorry was on railway property, and had stopped immediately across a railway-line, on a bend in the route. A train was approaching at high speed.

Leonard awoke lying on the ground, unable to see properly,

just aware that the lorry was upside-down near him, and burning briskly. An American soldier, drunk but concerned, was offering him wine from a straw-covered flask. Leonard next regained consciousness in a hospital. He was the sole survivor of the liberty-lorry, and he had barely survived. He had a fractured spine, a fractured skull, a broken jaw, a shattered nose – and he was blind. His eyes and hands were fully bandaged.

Leonard spent several weeks in a hospital in Algeria, experiencing to the full the panic and loneliness that besets men suddenly and terribly incapacitated. But it was here also that Leonard learned, by degrees and painfully, the benefits of mutual aid. In conversation he learned that the occupant of the next bed was an English sailor whose hands, arms and torso had been burned during a surprise air-raid. The sailor was unable to feel what he was touching. Leonard could assess what he touched, but was unable to see it. Within an hour the gunner and the sailor were able to feed one another with the food they required.

Then Leonard was transferred to a more advanced surgical unit, located in the Atlas Mountains. He discovered that the unit was staffed by surgeons rapidly becoming skilled in the relatively new techniques of plastic surgery. Bit by bit the fragments of glass and powdered metal were removed from his eyes, until at length the bandages were removed completely and Leonard was able to see again. What he saw gave him no initial confidence. He called for a mirror. After much delay and some whispered consultation a mirror was brought, and Leonard found himself looking into the eyes of a total stranger. The collision at Catania had utterly altered his facial structure. He shrank from his image as from some obscenity. The surgeons' task now was to restore his self-confidence, and to build him a new face.

The restoration took many months, but eventually Leonard was pronounced fit for extended convalescence in England. He sailed home in the *Capetown Castle*, and reached Southport in March 1944. After so long away from home the most rain-drenched fields seemed strange and totally beloved. Within a fortnight Leonard was allowed to go home. With his usual disregard for Army formality, Leonard decided to make his own way back to Huntingdon, and after some hours of hitch-hiking caught a bus that would take him to the familiar High Street and his mother's principal shop. In the bus he fell into conversation with an older man, a civilian and a farmer, who took pity on Leonard's battered condition, and talked intelligently about the progress of the war. In a sunny lane the farmer shook Leonard's hand, called, 'Good luck, soldier', and left the bus. Leonard sat for a few minutes, collecting his thoughts. The farmer had been one of his best customers for fifteen years, yet he had failed completely to recognize the new face of Leonard Wiles.

After a few months' convalescence, Leonard was summoned to Woolwich, judged unfit for further military service, and honourably discharged from the Royal Artillery. But although his active service was over by July 1944, the war itself proceeded, apparently undiminished. Leonard had gone into Woolwich to receive his civilian 'demobilization' suit, when a German rocket hit the town. Following the explosion, Leonard saw a man covered with soot and brick-dust lurching toward him.

'Come on, mate,' said the staggering man, 'you're out of all this rubbish now, and good luck to you. Tell us where you want to go and I'll bloody take you, if Jerry's missed my car.' Thus it was that Leonard Wiles returned to Huntingdon, and the problems of selling sweets, tobacco and cigarettes in a severely rationed England.

Concern for his mother kept Leonard in the confectionery business long after his interest in that way of life had waned. His long association with radio and radar had sharpened his pre-occupation with electronic engineering, and for some time he indulged this interest by repairing or building radio sets for friends and neighbours.

He felt the need to re-establish a life of his own, and decided that a car might be a beginning. Constant enquiries and many personal visits finally unearthed an ancient Rover with a fabric body – a vehicle that had been unused throughout the war. Leonard bought it for £50, stripped, examined and doctored the engine, reassembled it, and set out to recapture the youth that had somehow, unaccountably, passed him by. He was now thirty-five.

Two years later he was courting and having his first major row with his mother. She disapproved strongly of Leonard's choice. Leonard was determined on marriage, and came to realize that the only way to avoid everlasting dissension was to leave the confectionery business and strike out on his own. But in what direction? Leonard, now married, began to buy all the local newspapers and scan the advertisements for jobs that might suit him. Weeks passed, during which his never-large bank balance ran increasingly low, until he came across an advertisement by the Nene and Welland River Board for a Fishing Officer. Recalling his experiences with Grandad, and the hours spent angling for coarse fish, Leonard decided to try for the post. Technically he knew nothing about the job, and it was a considerable surprise when he was notified that he had been short-listed. Would he present himself for an interview at Peterborough Museum in a fornight's time? Leonard was excited, pleased, and appalled. He felt he had conned his way thus far, and could not honestly go forward to the interview in his present state of virtual ignorance. He besieged the local library and took out every book on the shelves on fishery, pollution and fishery protection. Smoking whatever cigarettes he could lay his hands on, Leonard did a fortnight's concentrated homework, then made his way to Peterborough Museum with justifiable tension. The interview was over before he had realized it had begun.

'Well now, Mr. Wiles,' his interviewer said, 'you've proved very fluent, very knowledgeable. Most encouraging. And a local man too. That helps, Wiles. Now look here, what we're going to do, we're going to put you on three months' trial.'

So for some years Leonard pursued the way of life that satisfied him most deeply, as an admixture of Water Bailiff, Piscatorial Adviser and Pollution Spotter. Every day carried its own problems. Every day Leonard was out and about in the milieu he loved – the world of practicalities and solitude, of sluggish tributaries and suddenly racing rivers; of water-meadows and Angling Contests and the ready give-and-take of the dedicated fisherman. There were only two clouds – but they were enough for Leonard. One was his deteriorating marriage, and the other was lack of money. The first he could do little about: his wife was a charming and capable woman, but she and Leonard, over a period of years, were getting nowhere with their relationship. Leonard was becoming less and less anxious to hurry home for dinner and conversation; his wife was sadly taking stock of the situation, and judging it doomed. Leonard recollected his mother's homilies, and realized, far too late. how sound her unwelcome advice had been.

But there were immediate financial matters to consider. By now, other River Boards were appointing officers whose duties corresponded precisely with those Leonard was discharging perfectly capably – and the new men were receiving far more money. Leonard, primed with precise figures, asked for equal pay. This was refused him. He resigned at once, and immediately re-applied for his old job, hoping thereby to satisfy his superiors' sense of the fitness of things. But the ploy did not work. For the first time since 1926 Leonard was out of work.

He tried a form of freelance fishery advising, but found the demand for his services too seasonal. The following summer he was penniless and without offers. His old preoccupation with the internal combustion engine revived, and Leonard quite suddenly wanted to do nothing more than to drive a heavy lorry. He could not justify this craving, merely acknowledge it. Without experience of anything heavier than cars, he felt his applications would fail – and they did. But one man evidently remembered Leonard's letter, and telephoned him quite unexpectedly one morning.

'Oh – Mr. Wiles? Look, I'm in a spot of bother . . . one of my chaps just up and left me without a moment's notice, and I've a lorry-load of vegetables to get to Liverpool. What about it?' Leonard weighed the proposition very briefly, then replied:

'Fine. I'll be along in twenty minutes.'

He turned up at the warehouse in his elderly Rover, and looked up at the 10-ton Commer, loaded with produce for the Liverpool markets. The boss strode across and shook his hand.

'Ah, Mr. Wiles. Leave your car here, eh? Got your driving licence handy? Good, good. Well, there she is – and here's the address . . . O.K.? Good luck.'

Leonard climbed into the cabin, waved to the boss, waited until he had disappeared into his office, then disembarked quickly and hurried away to get advice from another driver. After a few minutes' theoretical instruction, Leonard bounced the Commer out of the warehouse and set off for Liverpool, ears burning as he passed a traffic policeman on point duty in Huntingdon. There were several ugly, even terrifying moments for Leonard during the long haul west, but he arrived at the market intact, if a few hours late, and took a new load on for delivery in Huntingdonshire. Surging across quiet lanes on his way home the following morning, Leonard actually crowed with delight in the cabin of his very own lorry. This was total fulfilment, and no one would talk him out of it. Ever.

But as his satisfaction with and competence in his new career increased, his ability to hold the marriage together diminished. Tensions, long silences, a trial separation followed. Leonard, unused to failure, struggled to keep communication alive, but even at his most sanguine he was obliged to acknowledge that the relationship was damaging both to his wife and to himself. He took refuge in extra work, more driving. By now he had an old pick-up and a saloon car, but as his material prosperity increased he became more aware of the emotional poverty of his marriage.

One evening, working on a private commission, Leonard set out from Huntingdon for the American Air Force Base at Alconbury. A light rain was beginning to fall, and in his bleakest moments Leonard found himself missing the hard, bright air of the Libyan desert. Ahead of him, walking briskly down the road, were two girls – one blonde and petite, the other buxom and lively. Leonard slowed down until he was alongside them.

'Hello – where are you two off to?'

The girls looked at the pick-up with some hauteur, and at Leonard's battered, craggy face with more interest.

'Milsworth,' said the plump girl. 'We're going to the dance at the base and we missed the bus.'

'Hop in,' said Leonard, 'I'll take you as far as Alconbury.'

'You're on.'

The girls climbed in – the lively one sitting next to Leonard. The journey continued, and Leonard was soon chattering away in spite of his characteristic reticence – with the dark-haired girl next to him.

'Look here,' he said, 'it wouldn't be far out of my way if I was to drop you at the Brampton hut.'

'Terrific!' said the girls.

They reached the Brampton hut within twenty minutes.

'Now I'm here,' Leonard said, 'I might as well take you a little way up the Thrapston road.'

He continued driving, and returned to his animated conversation with the dark-haired girl on his left. They came to a public telephone kiosk. Leonard stopped the truck, made a brief telephone call, then returned.

'I'll take you into Thrapston,' he said.

They reached Thrapston as night fell, and Leonard drove to the nearest public house.

'What about a drink before you go on to the dance?'

The friends looked at one another, and the dark-haired girl replied, 'Plenty of time for a drink. Thanks.'

They moved into the bar, and Leonard bought drinks. And more drinks. He and the dark-haired girl dominated the conversation. The blonde friend was content to sip her gin and tonic and look brightly interested. At closing time the dark-haired girl said:

'We've been sitting here talking for almost four hours, but we don't know each other's names.'

'I'm Leonard.'

'Hello, Len,' said the dark-haired girl. 'I'm Hazel.'

CHAPTER FOUR

HAZEL

HAZEL was born by the light of a paraffin lamp inside a brightly painted, bow-shaped caravan in a field at Stanground, near Peterborough. It was 1930. The 'Leg of Mutton', as the caravan was called, sported a row of handsome brass holders on the steps and two great lanterns on the front to light the roads by night. But it was seldom used for travelling. Occasionally, the family would hire a horse and take off for the fair or another site. Most of the time, however, it would stand in Farmer Tonky Freeman's field alongside a dozen or more gaily decorated gypsy caravans. Not that Hazel's father was a gypsy; unlike his neighbours, he could make no claim to the famous gypsy family names of Deadman or McCoy. He worked as a setter in a local brickyard and even through the Depression of the 1930s, he was never out of a job. No one ever knew why he chose to live in a caravan, except that he was always out of pocket and eccentric in his tastes.

Harry Bird, 'Dicky' as he was known, was a quiet man with hazel eyes set in a round, gentle face. Only the military cut of his hair belied his otherwise mild appearance. He was a remote figure to Hazel as she grew up, a man forever ambling across the field in his cloth cap, muffler and baggy trousers. He did not treat her well, or badly: in fact he seemed to take no interest in her whatsoever. Many evenings he did not come home at all. Then Hazel was delighted. It meant that she could get to sleep without trying to block out the rasping voices of her mother and father as they bickered two feet above her head. For Hazel's bunk was directly under that of her parents and she would lie awake for hours, listening to their shouts, threats and abuse. The rows were always about one thing – money. Annie Bird would chide her husband for his lack of ambition. She wanted a home with proper furniture – a place to bring up her children. She was sick of the caravan and their gypsy way of life. What happened to the money he earned? What was he spending it on while his wife and child starved? On and on they would quarrel into the night, forgetting the plump little girl who lay scared and sleepless below them.

Annie Bird was the daughter of a Peterborough rag-and-bone man. She was a thickset country woman with red cheeks, twinkling blue eyes and curly hair. She, like her husband, had left school early and could barely read or write, but, unlike him she was ambitious and energetic. She was always washing, cooking, lighting the fires or chasing the dog or monkey. There was a continual struggle to keep clean, with no sanitation except the field, and one tap shared amongst the twelve families. The Birds' immediate neighbours had twenty-two children so there was always a scramble for water; yet however scruffy the children looked, or however much junk or scrap littered their pitches, the insides of the gypsy caravans remained spotlessly clean. Annie would scrape and scrub away the dirt, patiently boiling kettles on the small wood fire. 'Cleanliness is next to godliness,' she would repeat, until Hazel wanted to run into the field and dig up enough earth to bury both mother and caravan.

Bath-time happened once a week. A fire would be lit ceremoniously under the zinc bath which stood outside the caravan. When the water was hot enough the bath would be lifted gingerly inside and the family would take it in turns to have a dip.

The weekend bath ritual was followed by Saturday Hymns. Annie Bird was a keen Salvationist and every week the children were dragged in from the field to sing the same repertoire of old Salvation Army songs. The family now included Clifford, a red-haired, hot-tempered little boy, with whom Hazel soon came to live in open hostility.

When war came to Peterborough in September 1939, Hazel was nine years old. Even the huddle of caravans in Tonky Freeman's field had to be blacked out with sacking pinned to the doorway and over the skylight and air vents, making the interior unbearably hot. Already a nervous girl, Hazel was terrified when she was left alone and had to watch the black shapes of the unlit caravans suddenly and terrifyingly illuminated in the rays of the searchlight. The soldiers seemed to be playing odd, unfriendly games with the beam; sometimes it was so low that it would make her feet and legs a luminous white; sometimes it would be high and she could throw her pennies into the sky to catch the beam that turned them all to silver.

During those tense days at the beginning of the war, Hazel's sister, Jackie, was born in a friend's house, to the wail of a siren on the police station next door. Hazel, not guessing what the sound could be, wailed in return; but her sobs, the groans of her mother and the sharper cries of the new-born child were all drowned in that dreadful howl. She was convinced it was an evil omen: a noise like that at the moment of her sister's birth could only mean that from now on they were all doomed.

Two years later the war still raged, and life in the 'Leg of Mutton' did not improve. When Pat the youngest girl was born, Annie gave her ultimatum: 'I've scraped and scrubbed and looked after these damn children for going on twelve years,' she shouted at her husband, 'and what have you done? You bloody slipped off to your brother's fair and spent your money on booze instead of your family. Well, I'll tell you something. If you don't get us a house with a proper roof and four walls, I'm going to that fair and you can look after the children. And we'll see how you manage.'

Dicky Bird, frightened into action, found a thatched terraced house in John Street, near the centre of Peterborough, and the family moved in. Although there was no bathroom, no furniture and no electricity and they had to share beds, they were content. For once, they stopped their quarrels and set about making their first real home.

But the evil voice of the siren still haunted Hazel's twelve-year-old mind. Every time she heard it she remembered the terror of those hours in the strange house where her sister was born. As the war went on she became more and more convinced their good fortune would not last.

A few months after they moved in, the children and their mother were returning from a particularly successful shopping expedition. It was a windy autumn day and the air was already cold. They were not worried. Today the baby was in Hazel's arms and the pram was filled with lumps of shiny coal – this winter at least, they could look forward to warmth and a home. They turned the corner into John Street and noticed a crowd gathered opposite their house. Alarmed, they looked up and saw bright flames stripping the thatch and throwing clouds of burning straw into the sky. The fire brigade arrived but it was too late and within twenty minutes the whole house had burned down. Ironically, in the middle of a war, it had not been a bomb but a spark from a local bonfire which had blown into the thatch and set it ablaze.

In the ashes of the house lay all their belongings, their beds, clothes and a few pieces of furniture they had collected for the home. Hazel felt her heart crumple within her – she shuddered with cold and sickness. Flakes of burnt timber brushed like bats's wings against her cheeks as she choked on the smoke and her tears. She would remember this moment of horror thirty-two years later, in a context even more malign and destructive when Fate again played havoc with her most cherished possessions.

After the fire the family went to stay a few days with rag-and-bone relative, Grandfather Reynolds. The Mayor of Peterborough raised a disaster fund for the family, but during world upheavals people are not concerned with a small, natural disaster. Instead, the Council took them to a second-hand store where they acquired some stained mattresses, and showed them a condemned house where they could set up home for the second time. The house was in poor condition – the floorboards were falling in, the timber rotten and the window glass smashed – and it soon became too dangerous to occupy. The Birds decided they would have to move out and deliver themselves to the Workhouse.

For the first few days at the Workhouse the family were housed together, but when an outbreak of fleas occurred they were separated – mother and father in the main building and the children in the outhouses.

Hazel hated the Workhouse. The staff, she believed, were cruel, but careful to punish in a way that would leave no marks. Once she swore she heard the screams of a boy who had been forced to lie in a bath of ice. When she herself was naughty, they hit the soles of her feet with a hair-brush.

'Come on, Cliff,' she whispered to her younger brother, her feet still stinging from the blows, 'if we don't get away from here, they'll do us in. I'll meet you round the back five minutes after dinner, see? If you don't come, I'll give you worse than they ever done.'

It was not a dramatic escape, but it served its purpose. They ran to their grandfather's house and a few hours later their father arrived. Hazel was apprehensive. She had never rebelled like this before. But to her surprise her father – for the first and only time that she can recall – looked at her kindly and listened to her story. He took the triumphant girl and her brother and marched them back to the Master of the Workhouse. They had never seen their father so angry.

'What do you think you are doing?' he snarled at the Master. 'Your staff have whipped my daughter. Can't you see she's terrified? If you don't watch it, I'll report you to the police!' They left the Workhouse and went back to an irritated Grandfather Reynolds to beg a bed for the night.

During the war Annie Bird went to work on the railways, cleaning spare parts for steam engines, and Dicky Bird disappeared to London to work with the demolition squad; or more often, it seems, to escape to his brother's fair. Before leaving for London, he set up his family in a one-up, one-down cottage not far from their old home. Hazel would leave school every day and pick up her youngest sister from the nursery. Then she would go home, light the fires, clean the house, prepare the tea and wait for her mother's return. She begrudged the loss of her childhood. She hated lifting up the latch and walking into the cold, empty room; she resented the hours she spent tied to her baby sister while the others went out to play, and she dreaded the return of her mother who seemed to have grown even more indifferent and demanding as her family grew up.

There were no cuddles and kisses for the children. Annie Bird would laugh and joke with the neighbours, but reserved her hot temper for the home. 'If there was any loving,' Hazel was later to reflect, 'I should have known about it. But I can't remember her kissing us or anything like that. She could never even get our names right. If she wanted Hazel she would call for Jackie; if she wanted Pat she would shout for Clifford. I'm still known as Jackie or Pat.' Sex was never mentioned, and illness was taboo. There was never any time for Hazel to discuss her future or her school.

Hazel was no star pupil. She was considered backward, but because she did not cause trouble, she was put in the lowest class and left alone. She did not even have the advantage of an attractive appearance. A fat, plain girl with pigtails and glasses, she did not draw much attention to her problems, except for one embarrassing day in the gymnasium when they were forced to discuss her.

'Hazel Bird. Will you please do as the others and take off your dress!'

'I can't, Miss. I don't want to.'

'Hazel, you will do as you're told immediately or I'll remove it myself.'

Hazel did not reply. The teacher went to fetch a cane.

'For the last time, are you going to take it off or do you want a stroke of this?'

Terrified, Hazel blurted it out.

'I can't, Miss. Me Dad, he's gone to London and he don't send us money no more and me Mum, she works on the railways but she says she can't afford to buy me . . .' She turned red and stopped. '. . . pants!' she finally let out, and burst into tears.

The other girls giggled. She did not resist as the teacher removed her dress. She only looked with horror at the old combinations which she knew had been split down the back and fastened with a pin. The teacher summoned two colleagues, and for an hour the wretched girl was made to stand in her combinations in the corridor while they talked. She would never forget the humiliation she was made to feel that day.

Hazel left school at the age of fourteen, unable to read or write. She took up a job in a corset factory, but her eyesight, which had always been poor, could not cope with the fast machinery. She left to go into a laundry. There she did quite well, earning between £2 and £3 a week; and as the favourite of Wally, the manager, she soon rose through the ranks to the position of Chief Presser. Home life had also taken a turn for the better, at least as far as comfort was concerned. The war over, father returned and the family moved to the outskirts of Peterborough into one of the Nissen huts vacated by the Army. The hut was an improvement on anything they had known: there was a bathroom, boiler, cooker and most exciting of all, electricity. But they were still trapped by poverty. When there was a dance at the laundry and the other girls were discussing what they would wear, Hazel, who had to surrender her earnings to the home and had no suitable dress, pretended that she was too busy to go. Wally's wife however, guessing the problem, took her to the Peterborough Co-op and selected a dress in dark green taffeta with brown spots and a bow tie. Hazel could repay the debt later; in the meantime she could go with them to the dance.

It was about this time that she determined to teach herself to read and write. As the only member of the family who was completely illiterate, Hazel was used to asking the others to read out words for her. But one day her brother turned on her.

'You ignorant pig,' he shouted, 'I'm not going to tell you. You can bloody well go and find out for yourself!'

She did not know how to start learning the letters, but she remembered that the pub near their old house was called the Star Inn, and the words were written on a large sign that overhung the pavement. She walked to the pub, holding a notebook and pencil, and carefully copied the letters down. From then on, whenever she could, she copied words and asked what they meant until she had taught herself to read and write.

The two years at the laundry formed a relatively calm period in her life – a pause before the tide of disastrous marriages, broken affairs and children swept away in the squalls of her unhappy mistakes. Restless, ignorant, resentful of her poverty and the drabness that had always surrounded her, yet knowing nothing better, Hazel surrendered herself to every passing experience. Like every teenager she was searching for an ideal, a man who would lift her out of the messy confines of her life and who would give her dresses, diamonds and everlasting love. But the more desperate her attempts to raise herself to ladylike bliss, the more pitiful were the results. Hazel, uneducated, stubborn and deprived, had no more chance then of achieving her ambitions than a cart horse of running in the Derby. It was not until she was over thirty and secure in Leonard's care that she broke her pattern of falling clumsily into situations and as untidily running away.

Hazel's first husband, Bert Babcock, was a private in the Army. They met at the cinema where Hazel and a gang of girls would go to pick up the local boys. Bert had curly brown hair, bad teeth and a pleasant smile. He asked Hazel out for a cup of tea after the film and she accepted. They dated a few times and when he returned to barracks Bert, who was illiterate, asked a friend to write to Hazel. After a few months he proposed. His father, a tall, gaunt man who worked as a sorter in the Post Office, did not approve of the marriage or, it seems, of his son and offered Hazel £50 if she refused to marry him. 'If you make your bed, you lie on it,' he warned.

They married in the Register Office. She was seventeen and a half and he was two years older. Hazel's parents, who took even less interest in her now, did not appear; nor, of course, did Bert's father. But Hazel felt very grown-up. She wore a pale blue dress, a white hat, and blue and white sandals; around her finger was the coveted wedding ring. The wedding night was spent with mother-in-law in a red brick house in Peterborough. Their room was white-washed, with no furniture except for a double bed. A bare electric bulb hung from the ceiling. The honeymoon was not a success. Mrs. Babcock interfered with everything they did and soon made it clear that she had no time for the new addition to the household. Bert went back to camp and the two women were left to spend long, scratchy days in each other's company.

Hazel longed to go out, but if she did, Mrs. Babcock would be waiting to accuse her of 'going with other men'. She told her son that Hazel was being unfaithful, and when he was next home on leave he followed her about. One night she went with Bert's eighteen-year-old brother to the cinema. Bert had refused to come, but when the lights went on he was sitting behind them, scowling.

At home that night, Hazel, accused of corrupting her brother-in-law, received her first beating. They tried a reconciliation. Bert even suggested a holiday in Cornwall, and rented a room of their own in another town. But the truce did not last. They quarrelled and Bert struck Hazel, now seven months pregnant, in the the eye. She returned to her parents' home. A week before her eighteenth birthday, Karen was born.

Bert took compassionate leave but he did not visit Hazel or the baby. Instead, echoing cruelly the desertions of her father during the war, he disappeared with a travelling fair. The only visitors at the hospital were Hazel's mother and her brother who had been reluctantly dragged along and spent the visiting hour steadily eating the pomegranates he had brought.

A few weeks after the birth Hazel developed pleurisy and became seriously ill. Neither her mother nor father would take time off work to care for the baby. Instead they persuaded the pale, wheezing girl to a monstrous sacrifice.

'Why don't you write to Mrs. Babcock and ask her to come and help you? After all it's her grandchild, isn't it?'

'No Mum, I couldn't. You know what they're like. I don't want them touching Karen.'

'But you're sick, love. Heaven knows when you'll be up and about again. And who d'you think's going to feed and change her and wash her nappies? You're neglecting her, lying in that bed all day.'

'Now, there's a good girl,' her father joined in. 'You just write to Mrs. B and you'll see it'll be all right. It'll give you a chance to get better.'

Hazel, tearful, her lungs aching, was in no state to resist both her parents. She took the pen her father held out and shakily wrote the letter. Within a few days Mrs. Babcock came. Hazel could hear her parents and mother-in-law chatting and laughing in the kitchen, pouring out more and more cups of tea. She held on to Karen and muffled her sobs in the baby's shawl.

'Hazel!' her mother called. 'Bert's Mum is here. She says she can look after Karen for a few weeks. . . .'

It was the last time that Hazel held her daughter in her arms. A month later, still weak and depressed after her illness, she was standing outside Peterborough County Court.

'Now, Hazel,' she heard her mother's voice through the faint siren noises in her ears, 'whatever the man says, you say "Yes". Do you understand?'

She had no idea what was happening except that Mrs. Babcock had written a letter to her parents and that a lady had come to the house to ask them questions. She wanted her baby and she had been promised that if she did what she was told she would have Karen again. The Court was cold. Voices boomed and echoed in the stone gallery where she sat crouched beside her parents. Mrs. Babcock, thin-lipped in a new black suit, was standing below them in a box. Hazel could not catch all that she was saying but she heard her describe the red brick house where they had spent so many unhappy days. Eventually her own name was called. A man with a wig and black cloak led her into the box. Terrified, the sick, ignorant girl answered 'Yes' to all their questions. At the end, the Judge turned towards her and said that she could visit her daughter once a week. She wept. She did not understand how or why it had happened, but she knew she had lost her child.

Having recovered from her illness and the shock of the day in the County Court, Hazel plunged into a series of jobs – casual labour on farms, serving in cafés or, when her parents locked her out, residential jobs in restaurants and hotels. She was nineteen. She had lost everything – her husband, her child and her self-respect. She drank heavily, scrounging from anyone whom she could waylay, and looked around for another man.

Rick was a lorry driver, fair and muscular, with wide blue eyes. She was infatuated with his strong looks and considerate manner. She felt sure he would offer her the stability she needed, and take on his solid shoulders the disasters of her past. After all, he already took great pains to protect her – when they were travelling to London he would make sure to stop at a Ladies so that she could wash and brush up; he bought her a sleeping bag so that she could sleep in comfort in his unloaded lorry, and he would make sure that she had enough rest before returning home. Hazel, who had never been treated with such care, secure and close in the back of the parked lorry, offered herself whole-heartedly to him. Three months later, she knew she was pregnant and she wrote to tell him of the child. If he wanted her she would be glad to see him; if he didn't want to know then it would be better if he stayed away. Rick, who she later discovered was already married, took the predictable course. She did not see him again.

Hazel adored her second daughter. She had Rick's blonde hair and her own black eyes. She took her home, but her parents did not want the baby and did not believe that their unstable daughter was fit to bring her up. One night when the baby was a few weeks old, Hazel slipped out of the house to buy some cigarettes. At the pub she met some old friends and stayed to chat. Towards eleven o'clock she rushed back home only to find the doors locked and her parents shouting at her through the keyhole. She wandered about all that night, bewildered but not too upset. It was not the first time they had closed their doors against her. She walked to a transport café where she had once served and drank a cup of tea, then hitched a lift part of the way home. As the daylight spread through the grey swamps of sky and across the flat, misty fields, she thought about what she should do. She would find a job where she could take the baby and she would stop drinking. She wondered whether Rick would come and see his daughter. If he did, she felt sure he would look after them both as he had looked after Hazel before. She arrived home, her feet wet and her body aching with cold. The doors were still locked and the curtains drawn. It looked strange, like a house that has been boarded up and deserted years ago. Outside the front door on the gravel, her daughter's pram lay upside down.

For the second time, her child had been taken away. During the night her parents had got in touch with the local child care authorities and told them that she was incapable of looking after the baby. This time there were no court scenes. Annie Bird filled in forms and whenever anyone called, she spoke quietly on Hazel's behalf. Hazel was allowed to see her daughter once more – when she was beginning to walk. From that day on she was forbidden to know what was happening. The little girl was fostered, and Hazel believes that now, a beautiful young woman of twenty-four, she lives not far from Huntingdon.

Hazel was destroyed. Her early twenties passed in a succession of jobs, men and heavy drinking. She became a familiar figure astride the local bar stools, bantering with the men and joining in the sing-songs.

'Hi! Miss Hazel. What can I get you tonight?' She recognized the thick European accent. Karl was Rumanian, twenty years her senior, with stiff, thinning hair brushed back from a sallow forehead. He had fled to Britain during the war and had taken a job in a local brick-yard. They had met before and exchanged a drink and a chat, but tonight he was watching her with new enthusiasm. At closing time he offered to escort her home. They climbed in his old Morris and drove towards the café where she had taken a room and a job. A few months later they were married. Hazel was not in love, but she would make do with anyone who was kind and gave her security, and Karl had his moments of charm. Hazel, on the other hand, with her untidy ways and masculine habits, fell far short of his ideas about the rôle of women. She could never understand why he had wanted to marry her. Gradually she learned the bitterness of living with someone with whom closeness and mutual comfort was impossible, and within a year they separated. A few months later Karl was dead – crushed by a hopper at the brick-yard.

Hazel, finally convinced that Fate was against her, lapsed into another period of instability. She was twenty-seven, divorced and widowed, and had had two children taken from her. She had allowed the stains of her miserable childhood and girlhood to spread into her adult life. She had been on the verge of several breakdowns before and felt herself yet again dissolving into unproductive despair.

As usual when she was down, Hazel compensated with fun and friends. Depression, she realized, was unbecoming, especially in a 14-stone girl who enjoyed a laugh and a pint. There was a dance on at the Air Force base at Alconbury, and she and her friend Anne decided they would go. The two girls set off eagerly down the road to Brampton. They had missed the bus and would have to rely on a car or a lorry to give them a lift. Chatting and giggling, they casually waved their thumbs at any passing motorist. An old pick-up truck pulled into the side of the road in front of them, and a man with a weathered face and an amused expression wound down the window.

'Hello!' he said. 'Where are you two off to?'

CHAPTER FIVE

LEONARD AND HAZEL

'WE'VE been sitting here talking for almost four hours, but we don't know each other's names.'

'I'm Leonard.'

'Hello, Len,' said the dark-haired girl. 'I'm Hazel.' Leonard shook hands with both girls, then went off to his truck, and to Alconbury.

Hazel and Anne had missed the dance, and were now concerned with getting home. Anne was understandably anxious to know why Hazel had chosen to waste the evening in Len's company: 'He must be forty if he's a day.'

'You know who he is though, don't you?'

'No, I don't know who he is.'

'He's Leonard WILES. You know, Wiles that keeps the two shops in Huntingdon!'

'Oh. That Wiles. . . . But he's married, Hazel!'

'Yes, but it's different.'

'What do you mean, different?'

'He's a gentleman, isn't he? Not like the fellers you generally get giving you lifts. He wasn't after anything!'

'Yes, well, you can forget him, can't you?'

But Hazel was unable to forget Leonard quite as readily as her friend had advised. To her, Leonard represented all the things she felt were lacking in her own life: courtesy, education, style – and kindness. And in the weeks that followed, though Hazel made no attempt to put herself in the way of meeting Leonard, she did not avoid Huntingdon. One evening Leonard saw her gazing busily into a shop window. He crossed the road and spoke to her. Hazel feigned surprise and delayed recognition, but both of them were aware that this was not a chance meeting.

'In my Fishery days,' said Leonard, 'I invented what I think was rather a clever fish trap. Would you like to see it?'

'Now I've heard everything,' said Hazel, and they both laughed.

'Seriously, though . . .'

Leonard drove Hazel to a quiet place known locally as Whitewaters. They parked the car and went to the river, where Leonard had a boat moored. He rowed Hazel across to the trap. There was nothing in it. They laughed again, and fell silent. Both of them recognized the excuse for a chance to be alone together. In the thickening dusk they revealed the inadequacies of their lives: Hazel's bewildering heartbreaks, the aridity of Leonard's own relationship. By the time they went back to the car they knew they were in love. Somehow they would see one another again.

They met a few more times for a drink at the Royal Oak in Huntingdon, but Leonard was married and did not seem in a hurry. Hazel, still bitten by memories of Rick, decided to keep away.

She took a job in the cafeteria at the Alconbury base, and it was there that she met Roger. He was a pale, skinny boy who worked in the barracks and lived with his mother on the base. He was attracted by Hazel, and when she told him her problems of getting home after a late night shift, he persuaded her to live with them. He became more and more attached to the older, more extrovert girl and demanded that Hazel should marry him. As with her first marriage, Fate gave her adequate warning against the marriage. She went to her doctor in Huntingdon to fetch a presciption and mentioned her plans to marry.

'Pack your bags if you know what's good for you and leave that house!' he said with unusual vehemence. 'I know Roger and his mother, and I'll tell you this much: if you stay there. you'll be dead within a year.'

But Hazel's stubborn desire for a partner and a home drove her on. After her visit to the doctor, she wandered about the shops in the town, half-hoping to see Leonard, from whom she hadn't heard for months. She was in luck. She saw his big, untidy figure coming out of the door of Barclay's Bank. They collided.

'Hello,' he said casually, as if they were meeting after a day's separation. 'How're things down at Alconbury?' Hazel told him bluntly about Roger's offer of marriage. Leonard looked at her thoughtfully.

'Well, good luck!' he said. 'It sounds as though you've got a nice young man to take care of you. Come and see us some time.' Hazel was stunned. As he walked away, apparently unconcerned that he was losing her for good, she made up her mind. She would marry Roger, despite the doctor's warning.

Ironically, the wedding to Roger was the most memorable of the three. She wore lilac and felt very gay. All Roger's workmates were there, wine and beer were plentiful. and the reception lasted into the next day. But it was only a few hours after signing the book that Hazel came across her first shock. Although his friends joked pleasantly about it, she discovered that Roger had told them he was marrying a blonde, a model who worked in London. He had even cut out photographs from a fashion magazine to show off his imaginary beauty to the other men.

This was the beginning of her nightmare. Over the next few weeks she discovered that Roger lied about almost everything – he seemed unable to distinguish between fact and fantasy. The longer she lived with him the more certain she felt that without the elaborate, exciting structure of lies on which he built his life he was lost. They were as essential to him as food. There was something strange in the dark eyes of the mother's boy who had become her husband. He seemed to her like a shadow, distorting all truth, stretching or shrinking in the brightness of some weird, inner sun. She began to understand what the doctor had meant, and she was afraid.

One day Leonard contacted Hazel without preamble.

'I'm going to an RA reunion on Saturday night in London. Want to come?'

'I wasn't in the Artillery, Len.'

'You know what I mean!'

'O.K. I'll come.'

They arranged to meet outside a bank in Huntingdon on the Saturday morning. Hazel was dressed and ready a few minutes before the appointed rendezvous. She was suddenly very nervous and felt utterly inadequate. She could not believe that such an outing would actually happen. Nervously she paced up and down outside the bank, past a smart car and a well-dressed driver.

'Are you getting in, or not?' said Leonard.

Hazel stopped short on the pavement.

'Len – it's you!'

Leonard in a white shirt with a stiff collar and a regimental tie. Leonard in a dark suit and highly polished shoes. Leonard in a new car, gleaming with polish. Hazel felt very young and inexperienced. She climbed into the car, and Leonard drove south.

Shortly after noon he suggested they should stop somewhere for lunch. Hazel demurred. Leonard drove on, assuming that she was not yet hungry. The real reason for her apparent lack of appetite was her fear of making a fool of herself in front of him, in the kind of hotel to which he was clearly accustomed. She foresaw endless embarrassments over the choice of food, the selection of the correct cutlery for each course, the confusion if a menu were presented to her in French. Starvation would be preferable to a social disaster such as this.

At Baldock, Leonard drove to the forecourt of a hotel and suggested they should have a drink together, at any rate. He ordered drinks, and Hazel's fears were allayed. Then she realized that Leonard had ordered a table for two in the hotel, and that it was too late to invent excuses for not eating. The head waiter summoned them into the dining-room, and Hazel's most extreme fears were justified. Here was the world of opulence and *savoir-faire* – of formally dressed waiters in bow ties, with napkins over their arms, and surely a score of them dancing attendance around their table. Hazel perched uneasily on the edge of her chair, blindly staring at the gleaming silver before her. Leonard asked for the wine waiter. Briefly, the two were without hotel assistance. Leonard leaned forward and said to Hazel:

'Do you know what these waiters remind me of?'

Startled, Hazel looked about her.

'No. What?'

'They look exactly like unemployed Presbyterian ministers.' Hazel began to laugh, and the ice was broken.

When Leonard returned to the London hotel after his reunion dinner he joined Hazel for drinks, and they sat together for hours, attempting to decide what they could best do about their future. By then life apart from one another seemed impossible, yet both were still committed elsewhere, however unsuccessfully. They drove back to Huntingdon very early on the Monday morning, since both had to be at work by nine at the latest.

Leonard came to collect Hazel from work two evenings later. By now Hazel was careless of gossip. She ran up to him, then hesitated. His face was grave and drawn. He appeared not to have slept for nights.

'It's no good going on like this,' he began.

'I see. You want us to stop seeing each other?'

'No. I think we should get out from under and start living together.'

'You mean it?'

'Of course I mean it – we're never going to be happy unless we do.'

And now it was Hazel who was reluctant, uncertain. So radical a move so early in the game appalled her. She thought of the arguments, the tears, the recriminations that would lie ahead – for both of them. She began to temporize. But Leonard was adamant. For him it had to be a deliberate and formal declaration of their love for one another, or an end to their relationship. Hazel begged for a little time to consider the implications.

'We've considered them already,' he pointed out. 'We've talked of nothing else.'

It was time for Hazel to face Roger. He was waiting for her – tense, nervous but aggressive. He exploded the alibi she had provided for her weekend with Leonard, and accused her, not without justification, of humiliating him by her behaviour. The recriminations began. Hazel compared the behaviour of this neurotic creature, screaming and actually rolling on the floor, drumming his heels against the door with rage and frustration, with the self-assurance and stability of Leonard.

'I'm sorry, Roger,' she said. 'We both made a terrible mistake when we got married, and staying together's going to destroy us both.'

She packed stolidly to an accompaniment of tears and oaths.

'Goodbye. I won't be coming back.'

She went off to meet Leonard. He hired a caravan, and they moved in together.

It was an irrevocable action for both of them, but both were overcome with feelings of guilt; each felt responsible for having broken up the other's marriage. They had presented their friends with a *fait accompli* and they intended to make it successful. They talked endlessly, rationalizing, explaining, consoling. Should they have children? Leonard's marriage had been childless, and he would clearly love to have a son or daughter of his own by Hazel; Hazel had two children whom she was now no longer able to see, and she had doubts. But the discussion turned out to be academic. Hazel went to the doctor who confirmed a hidden fear: because of an operation shortly after her second child was born, the chances of Hazel's having further children were negligible. She would have to reconcile herself to that fact as soon as possible. Forlorn daydreams would ruin her relationship with Leonard more surely than the absence of children of their own.

Their life together continued, not always easy, but always more acceptable than the lives that they had led before. As soon as both were free, Leonard and Hazel married. Hazel was still jumpy and over-emotional, and would occasionally explode into acts of anger and frustration. Once the two of them had a prolonged row, which ended in Hazel's hurling a dinner set across the caravan at Leonard. Straight-faced, he dodged the attack, then bent forward and picked up a gravy-boat, the only object left intact. He walked across to the weeping Hazel and presented her with it formally.

'Here you are, Ma'am,' he said. 'It's the only one we have, but it's a good one.'

Hazel stared at him blindly for a moment, then collapsed into laughter, in which Leonard joined. Gradually, Hazel's jumpiness began to subside, though she was still wretched when his lorry-driving kept him away from her for more than a couple of nights at a time.

One morning in the summer of 1966, Leonard was returning home from Edinburgh, his lorry heavy with ten tons of paper. Just south of Catterick another lorry overtook him on a bend and cut in so sharply that Leonard was faced instantaneously with the choice of ramming his tailplate or leaving the road. He spun the wheel and fought to avoid the vehicle ahead, then saw a telegraph pole on the bank. The impact jerked his load forward, and the cab twisted and tore as bales plunged through its roof. Leonard was stunned. As he recovered consciousness he realized he was trapped, hardly able to breathe under the weight of paper on his back and shoulders, unable to move, except for his right hand which hung incongruously out of the window.

The other lorry had gone on its way, unaware of the havoc a careless move had made. It was two hours before police and helpers had released Leonard from the buckled cabin, and he was rushed to the army hospital in Catterick. His injuries were serious. His back and shoulders were torn and bruised, and the base of his skull was fractured. His head was shaved so that doctors could work on his broken skull. For a month he lay on his hospital bed, head on one side, suffering terrible headaches.

Slowly the damage mended and eventually he was well enough to return to Hazel and the caravan. He was eager to resume lorry driving.

But it was not to be as simple as that. Not long after he had started work again he had a blackout. It happened again and again, and Leonard realized he could not safely continue to drive. The specialists found the trouble – the accident had made his pancreas over-active. After two years and two operations, he was cured. But from now on heavy lorries were forbidden. Only light work would do.

Feeling wretched, Leonard paid his first visit to the local Employment Exchange. The officials were helpful and told him to go out to Brampton Nurseries, where there was a vacancy for a van driver. Leonard took the first available bus, and met the managing director. He interviewed Leonard, but felt he must reserve judgement until Leonard had met the nursery foreman. Leonard paced up and down outside, smoking nervously. He and Hazel had absolutely no money and several debts. If he did not get this job he would be in considerable difficulties. The foreman appeared and, to Leonard's relief, he was a Huntingdon man who had known Leonard almost all his life. The job was secure. Leonard was mainly to drive the van, but occasionally there would be hauls in a 3-ton lorry. He took the bus back home, and celebrated his new-found employment with Hazel on a great blow-out of beer and fish and chips.

Throughout the autumn Leonard drove his van without difficulty, although his back, injured first in Sicily and again at Catterick, caused him considerable pain from time to time. But as the weather deteriorated, driving conditions became more hazardous and Leonard's journeys away from home became longer. One night he drove back from Eastbourne in a blizzard, and arrived at the caravan bitterly cold and exhausted. There were no lights anywhere. Leonard wearily entered the caravan and found Hazel, covered with all the blankets she could find, shuddering with cold.

'There's no electric,' she said. 'The lines must be down.'

'Then what about a cup of tea?'

'There's no water.'

'What d'you mean – no water?'

'Pipes are frozen.'

'Oh my God. Then what about the fire?'

'Calor gas is frozen as well.'

'And this is just the beginning of winter!'

Leonard took off his shoes and crawled into bed, teeth chattering and fingers numbed.

'We'll die,' he said, after a while, 'if we have to go on like this.'

Hazel shivered.

'Where else can we go?'

'We need somewhere where we can have a coal or wood fire.'

'Good thinking, Len! What about Buckingham Palace! Meantime, we're stuck with this caravan.'

'There's just one chance,' he said.

The following morning, instead of loading up his van, Leonard went to see the manager of the Nurseries.

'There's a couple of Nursery Cottages still empty.'

'Used to be. But one of them's taken. Len Curry's moved in there.'

'What about the other one?'

'It's a mess, you know, Len. Hasn't been lived in for years.'

'It has a roof and four walls, doesn't it?'

'Yes, but . . . it's nothing to write home about.'

'I need it, for Hazel and me.'

'Well, I don't know . . .'

'Look, if we stay in the caravan much longer in this weather we'll be down with pneumonia. What good will I be if I'm in hospital?'

'Tell you what, I'll see what I can do. I'll have to square it up with the owners in London.'

'We've got to move today, or I'm quitting.'

'All right then. Move in this evening. But keep it quiet until I've sorted it out with the owners.'

During Leonard's lunch break he motored into Huntingdon and bought a second-hand bed. Hazel found three orange-boxes, and by evening, as snow began to fall even more heavily, they moved to Nursery Cottages.

The small group of buildings of which the cottages formed part stood perhaps a hundred and fifty yards off the Thrapston road, up a pitted cart-track. When Leonard and Hazel bounced and slid up the frozen track through thick snow Hazel looked up and blinked.

'*Len!* There's a fire going!'

They pulled up outside the cottage, and found that their new neighbour, Len Curry, had got a wood fire burning in their living-room grate. Len Curry was chief repair mechanic at the Nurseries. and he and Leonard had struck up a quiet friendship. Len Curry helped them to carry in the bed, blankets and orange boxes. Hazel was reluctant to hunt about upstairs.

'It's warm here,' she said. 'We'll live here until we get some more furniture.'

They boiled some soup, and squatted in front of the fire on their orange boxes. They had no money, no fuel, a handful of cigarettes, and a winter to live through, but when Len Curry had wished them good night and gone back to his cottage, Hazel threw her arms round Leonard and hugged him, crying a little.

'It's our first real home,' she said, 'and it's beautiful.'

Somehow they managed to get through the freak cold spell. The snow disappeared, and by November fog lay thick on the low ground and meadows which spread beyond their cottage. One afternoon Leonard returned from a long haul in the south of England to find Hazel very thoughtful and sombre.

'I'm worried, Len,' she said.

Earlier that day she had opened the cottage door to find an elderly couple, who appealed to them for help. Their daughter, Hazel's friend, had given birth to a baby born without limbs. The shock had been too much for the girl. She was advised never to see him again. The child, now five, was safely installed in a hospital, but he needed a guardian, someone who could sign papers and deal with formalities. The old couple felt they were too old to carry that burden, and no one else in the family would take on the responsibility.

'You are her best friend, Hazel. Won't you and Len help? Will you be Andy's guardian?'

'I'll have to talk to Len,' she said.

Over supper Leonard tried to think it out.

'Hazel, the old people aren't asking us to do very much, are they? Simply means that if your friend's child needs any more operations they'll come to us for permission. What is there to that?'

'I don't want to see him, Len. I never want to see him.'

'Neither do I. And there'll be no need. All we have to do is to be here in case there's an emergency, and the doctors will know who to talk to.'

'Well,' said Hazel, 'If that's all it means, then all right – we'll think about it. But no fast decisions. We need time to think it over.'

Leonard privately decided that when next he had the opportunity, he would visit the boy, and talk to the hospital authorities. That would help him to make up his mind one way or another.

PART TWO

Living Together

CHAPTER SIX

WHERE DO WE GO FROM HERE?

DISTANTLY, Andy was bellowing at them. Hazel and Leonard moved down the ward. The bright brown eye regarded them earnestly.

'I'm coming to the cottage, aren't I – at Whit? I can see all the places you've told me about!'

They walked across to the lorry.

'I can't, Len. I can't, it's impossible. What's the use of getting dragged into something when we know there's nothing we can do?'

'Give it time,' he urged. 'Just give it time.'

All the way home, and at home, they tossed the idea back and forth. They had no idea how they could handle such a situation as Chailey was proposing. A few hours in the middle of the day – fair enough, they thought. But to have such a badly disabled child around the house for five solid days! Although they were quite without experience of coping with handicapped people of any sort, they were being asked to entertain an almost impossible case. No, no. A visit – yes, but having him at home – no. Not really.

The matter seemed to be settled within a couple of days. But a week later Hazel and Leonard were chewing it over once more, unable to leave it alone. Is it fair, they thought, now that he's met us, to let him stay behind at Chailey when probably most of the other children will have something to look forward to at Whit?

'It's not as though he was mentally backward, or anything like that,' Leonard argued. 'He's a bright little boy – plenty to say for himself. And you saw how he handled that meal on his own. It won't be so bad, really. It can't be. And anyway, it's only for five days.'

Hazel agreed, but made one stipulation:

'I don't want him getting fond of us, Len, or there'll be all kinds of trouble and unhappiness. And I'm not going to get involved with him. We've got problems of our own, haven't we?'

Andy's visit to the cottage at Whitsun 1968 was a total disaster. Hazel and Leonard, by nature demonstrative and kindly, seemed unable to break through the bitterness and reserve which Andy carried with him like a shield. He would not respond to Hazel's attempts to cuddle and kiss him. He flinched from overt affection, and would remain standing absolutely still in the living-room in his artificial limbs. At one stage Hazel, desperate to reach him, asked him why he was suddenly so difficult and tense. Gradually the child revealed that he believed that he had been sent to Chailey as a punishment for possessing no limbs. Hazel and Leonard, over-compensating in an effort to make him feel wanted, soon found themselves at his beck and call from seven in the morning until ten at night. He wanted a drink; he needed to go to the lavatory; he wanted to go into the field; he wanted to come back. He wanted his artificial limbs on; he was frightened of his artificial limbs; he wanted to watch television – where was the television? Could he have some sweets? No, not those sweets, the other sort – the sort that Elizabeth always gave him.

After three days of competing with Elizabeth both Leonard and Hazel were exhausted and cantankerous. Leonard had some kind of excuse to get away, since a morning's job was proposed, and Leonard needed the money. Hazel was left alone with this twenty-one-inch tyrant, and she doubted if she would last the morning out.

The moment Leonard left the cottage, Andy began his onslaught of demands. He wanted to play with Sheba the dog. He was frightened of the dog. Could he sit in a chair? He wanted to roll on the floor. Could he have some crayons? Where was the red crayon? This paper was no good – Elizabeth always gave him proper paper. During all this time Hazel was running into the living-room from the kitchen where she was attempting to prepare lunch. The twentieth demand from the tiny creature in the next room snapped her tremulous patience entirely. She rushed through and saw Andy rolling about on the floor, saying it was time for his orange drink. Hazel picked him up and shook him vigorously, then tossed him on to the bed in the corner of the room.

'You horrible, selfish little boy!' she shouted. Andy struggled to sit upright, and eased his glasses back on to his nose with his shoulder-blade.

'What's the matter?'

He was clearly amazed and frightened. Hazel, large and formidable in rage, advanced on him and scowled down.

'I am trying,' she said, 'to get two meals ready. I am going to spend the next hour in the kitchen *uninterrupted*. And if I hear another squeak out of you, there'll be trouble.'

Andy nodded.

'Will you just put me on the floor please?'

'I will. And that's the last thing I shall do for you until I'm ready to come through!'

Hazel propped Andy up against an orange box and left him to his own devices. She raged into the kitchen and oversalted the potatoes, then went out into the lane to cool down. Her hands were shaking, and she wanted to be sick. 'When Len comes home,' she thought, 'we are taking that child straight back to Chailey. Or I leave.' Then she returned to the kitchen and the potatoes.

After a time she saw that Andy had wriggled forward on his buttocks from the centre of the living-room to the kitchen doorway.

'Mum,' he said.

'Be quiet, Andy. And I am not your Mum.'

'Sorry.'

Andy remained propped against the door jamb while Hazel moved from one room to the other, tidying up, writing a letter, hurrying back to the kitchen to check on the cooking.

'I've got something for you,' Andy said timidly.

Hazel looked down. There was a folded piece of paper projecting from his left flipper.

'Well, it'll have to wait, won't it?' she said.

Andy did not demur. Deliberately Hazel set herself to keeping the boy waiting. He would have to learn who was boss or she would go under. Finally she wiped her hands on a towel and said, 'All right. I have a bit of time. What is it?'

'It's a note.'

Hazel bent down and took the piece of paper from him. She opened it. In large, ungainly scrawl was a single sentence, one that Andy had taken twenty minutes to write with his flipper: 'I love you Mummy.'

Hazel went outside, across the lane and into the field, and cried.

When she was under control she was determined not to let Andy see how he had affected her. 'This is another ruse,' she argued. 'A way of apologizing and buttering me up. He has to learn he can't get away with things quite so easily.' But after lunch the child struck home again. As Hazel was washing up, Andy shuffled into the kitchen to watch her. After a time he said, 'When my arms grow I'll be able to wash up for you, won't I?' It took a few seconds before the implications of this remark became fully clear to Hazel. She crouched down beside him.

'What did you say?'

'I said that when my arms grow I'll be able to do your washing-up, won't I?'

'Andy, who told you your arms would grow?'

'One of the nurses.'

Hazel stood up. Her hands were quivering.

'Andy,' she said, 'your arms will never grow. If you'd been meant to have arms you'd have had them when you were a baby.'

'But I've got little holes in my shoulders, haven't I? That's where my arms will come from.'

'Andy – you are never going to have arms of your own, and you must understand that now. I mean it. You'll have to find other ways of doing things for yourself.'

When Leonard returned he found Andy quietly drawing, and Hazel in a sombre mood. When Andy had been put to bed Hazel revealed the reason for her tension.

'I don't want any more moments like that,' she said. 'Why did it have to be me to tell him he'd never have arms?'

The last full day of Andy's first visit occurred on a Tuesday, when both Leonard and Hazel were due back at the Nurseries. At this time Hazel was also temporarily employed as a van driver there, and Andy was anxious to see where she was working. Hazel's colleagues had been told that he might be coming along, and had been warned by both Leonard and Hazel about his disabilities. Consequently when Hazel first arrived, carrying Andy, the other girls bent their heads in an excess of tact and began to transfer plants into boxes. Andy watched for a long time in silence, then asked one of the girls why she was taking plants from the earth to put in boxes, where they would surely die. The girl explained that the only way to carry plants from one part of the country to another was to put them in boxes first.

'But if they're all jammed in lots of boxes and put in lorries and trains, won't the plants die by the time they get to the other end?'

Recognizing the six-year-old logic of the question, the girl explained that the plants were kept moist and therefore healthy because wet moss was placed round their roots. This answer satisfied Andy, and almost at once his attention was caught by the activities of another of the girls, and he began talking to her animatedly. At the end of the morning, when Hazel had seated Andy in her van, two of her friends called her over to them.

'We were a bit nervous, Hazel,' one of them said, 'when you told us Andy was coming up here for a bit. We didn't think we'd be able to talk to him, and we didn't want to be staring at him all the while. But he's bright, isn't he? He chatters away there just like any other kid. Makes you forget he's ... got problems.'

That evening, when the time had come for Leonard to return Andy to Chailey, Hazel attempted to cuddle and fuss him – to take him in her arms as might any mother with a small child being returned to prep school. But Andy backed off, went stiff, and would not respond. He disliked being kissed, and would show no outward signs of affection. It occurred to Hazel, not for the first time, that Andy was using them simply as a means of escape from Chailey, and not from any instinctive affection he might possess for them.

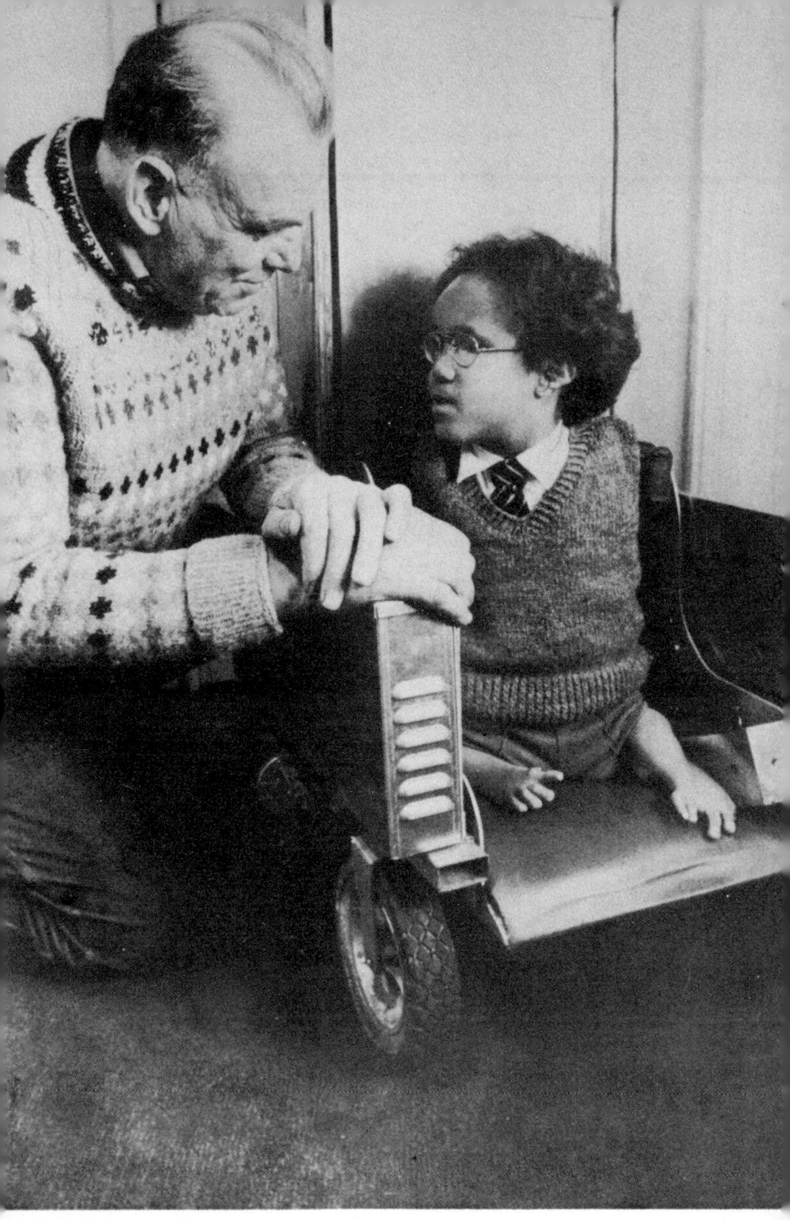

The Pioneers: Leonard and Terry work together on Supercar Mk I

'... He's a wonderful boy and he loves me and that makes me very proud.'

Caravan workshop: more inventions

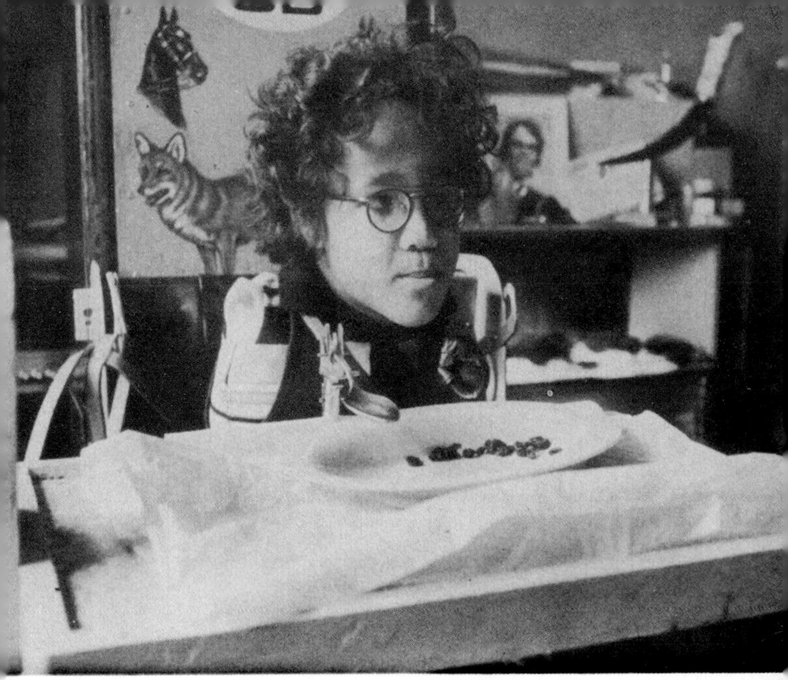

The eating miracle

King of the Road!

Enter Tracey – the pupil with two teachers

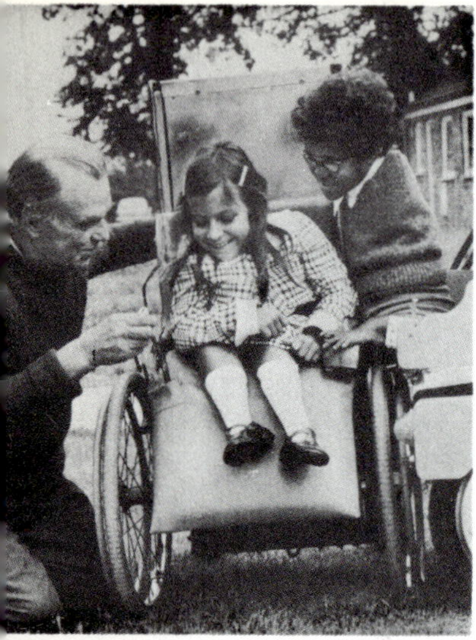

All my own work

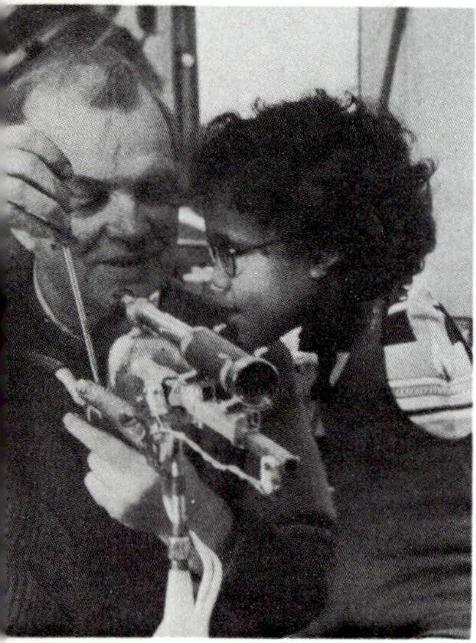

Building the telescope

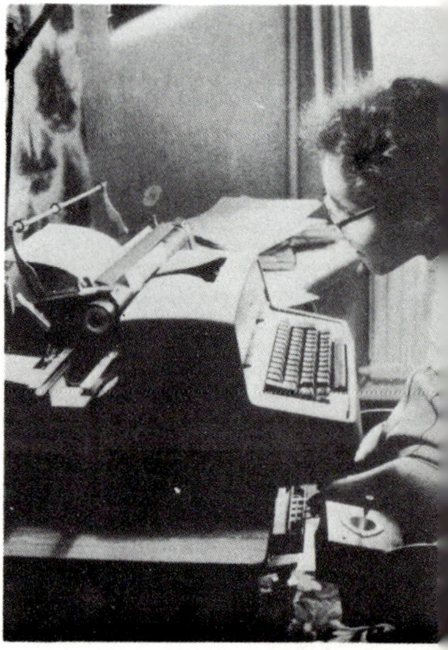

The treble miracle: Possum, the adaptation and Terry

When Leonard left him at Chailey later that night, Andy's last words were. 'I'm coming home for the summer, aren't I? You won't just go away and forget me, like the others?'

Hazel and Leonard had expected that with Andy no longer there, life at the cottage would resume its familiar relaxed orderliness. They would have time for one another again, and time for Sheba, whose nose had been radically put out of joint by the arrival of Andy. For a few days, Leonard and Hazel congratulated one another on not becoming too involved with the child, and attempted to lead a planned social life. But within a week they were looking at the calendar, marking off the days until they would have Andy with them again. Chailey had asked if they would like to have him for an entire fortnight, and this would pose certain problems. Both of them were still driving for the Nurseries, and it was clear that Hazel would have to ask for a fortnight off in order to devote her time to Andy. But a fortnight without Hazel's pay would damage their always slender financial resources. Neither of them the best of managers when it came to money, they were already in debt, and saw no hope of ever having a credit account at the bank. Yet all these worries were diminished by the growing excitement they both felt at the prospect of having Andy home again.

They set off early on a Sunday morning with Sheba, and motored down to Chailey in good weather. Their spirits rose with every mile that passed, and by the time they reached the hospital, they were unable to conceal their impatience to see the child. They were shown into the day-room. Andy stood in a corner, upright and immobile in his suit and artificial limbs.

'Hello, Andy!' they called, and crossed the room. Andy looked at them expressionlessly.

'Are we going home now?' he asked, without apparent interest.

His artificial limbs were in the boot of the car, and Andy sat in Hazel's arms as Leonard drove through the outskirts of London. In almost an hour's driving the child had not offered one comment of his own. His conversation was limited to terse replies to their questions only. Looking at the withdrawn, bitter little face, Hazel wondered how they would ever stand a fortnight of this intolerable atmosphere. The tiny helpless creature was dominating them effortlessly, and they could find no way to reverse his bleak withdrawal from their lives. In desperation Leonard decided to drive along the Embankment – anything in an attempt to distract the boy. Hazel and Leonard chatted desultorily, then Andy's excited voice cut across their conversation: 'What kind of ship is that, Mummy?'

Andy had returned to life.

Although they had promised the Chailey authorities that Andy would use his artificial arms and legs while he was at the cottage with them, Leonard soon realized the extent of the child's helplessness in this formidable apparatus. Within hours of the boy's arrival, Leonard and Hazel agreed that he should be left to develop what natural abilities he possessed. The arms and legs were put away, and Andy was set on the carpet to move about as he was able.

For the first time, Leonard and Hazel set themselves to observe him constantly, in an effort to understand what they might be able to do to make him less dependent upon the artificial limbs. It was Sheba who clinched their determination to abandon false hands. The dog, placid and faithful, lay sprawled in a corner of the room. Andy rolled over and over until he was close to her and rested his head against her flanks.

'Try to stroke her,' Hazel said.

Andy wriggled round, and patted the dog clumsily with his left flipper. Sheba looked up, yawned, and relaxed again.

'Do you realize this is probably the first time he's ever touched an animal in his life?' said Leonard. 'And he's six!'

The full enormity of Andy's situation was brought home to them even more forcefully by this simple situation. They realized that as long as Andy continued to use false hands, he would never have direct tactile contact with anything. He would never understand the feel of wood, of silks, of any materials, of human bodies, of animals, of grass, of flowers.

'It would be as if we could never use our hands, and had to pick up everything with a pair of tongs,' Hazel observed.

Within a few days Hazel was exhausted again. Andy, with or without artificial limbs, could never be left on his own for a moment. If Hazel propped him up against a wall, or the bed, Andy was in fear of falling over. Whenever Sheba came into the room and sniffed around him, he would scream for Hazel, frightened of being knocked over and of hurting his head. So one afternoon Hazel set herself, with complete concentration, to make him lose his fear of falling.

She spread a few blankets on top of the carpet, and set Andy down on his buttocks in the centre of the room. He could balance himself with his flippers. He looked up at her expectantly. What was this new game going to be?

'Right, Andy,' she said. 'You're frightened of falling over, aren't you?'

'Yes – you know I am.'

'Okay. I'm going to push you over.'

'No, Mummy, please don't.'

'I'm going to push you over. Now. Bang!'

As she said 'Bang!' she shoved him gently in the chest. He fell backwards on to the carpet, whimpering with fear. Hazel set him upright.

'And again. Bang!'

'Please. No.'

She set him upright again. 'Now listen: did you hurt yourself when you fell?'

'No.'

'Well then.'

'But I was frightened.'

'Why?'

'Frightened of hurting myself.'

'I'm going to push you over again – bang!'

'And again – bang!'

'And again – bang!'

For half an hour Hazel pushed the boy over, set him upright, and pushed him over again. At the end of that time he was pleading with her to stop.

'Andy,' she said, 'if other children fall over they can break the fall with their arms – right? But you have no arms – and if you were wearing your false ones they'd be no use either, would they?'

'No.'

'So – if you have no arms you have to think of some other way of breaking your fall.'

'But how? I just thump down.'

'Can you remember what you were trying to do those last few times I pushed you over?'

'No. I just didn't want to fall.'

'Stop saying that and just think.'

He was silent, and tearful. 'I don't want to fall over.'

'Right. Over you go – bang!'

'Over you go – bang!'

'Over you go – bang!'

She set him upright again. 'Stop scowling at me, and tell me what you were trying to do just then. Andy!'

'I was . . . trying to roll over on to my shoulder.'

'Why?'

'So my shoulder would hit the ground first.'

'Instead of what?'

'Instead of my face or head.'

'You want to protect your face and head. Why?'

'Because it hurts more if I bump my nose or head than if I fall on my shoulder.'

'Good. You started to lean and roll as you fell. Show me – I'll hold you this time.' Andy demonstrated his new-found technique.

'Very good. But when you fall, there won't always be someone to catch you, or let you down slowly. Come on. Over you go – bang! Over you go – bang! . . .'

After a further hour and a half, Hazel and Andy had together tried every variety of fall – frontal, backwards, and to the right and left. Andy was now able to assess how to turn and roll so as to land on his shoulder until he could swing and fall as gracefully as a sapling. Both of them were exhausted. Hazel cuddled him and made him a drink of orange juice.

'We'll have something to tell your Dad when he comes home,' she told him; then she realized what she had said. Andy sat on the floor, the glass between his teeth, grinning up at her. Hazel went into the kitchen quickly.

' "Tell your Dad"? Watch it, Hazel,' she warned herself.

Leonard was impressed and delighted with the progress

Andy had made, but when the child had been tucked into bed, he confided his fears to Hazel. 'So long as he's here with us, he can do far better without that contraption. But the moment he gets back to Chailey he's going to have to wear it again. And he spends far more time there than he ever could here.' He lit a cigarette and vanished into the kitchen. Three hours later he was still there. Hazel had fallen asleep, and now woke, wondering what he was doing. She padded into the kitchen. Leonard had laid out the artificial legs, and stripped them down.

'What are you doing, Len? Those things are expensive!' Unperturbed, Leonard was making a quick sketch on a torn cigarette packet.

'There must be a way of making it easier for him to walk in these things. You go to bed, eh? It's going to take some time.' Hazel went off to bed. Leonard lit his final cigarette and looked again at his sketch, and at the artificial legs. Since the late 1940s he had done no creative mechanical or electrical work – there had been no need.

In his time he had been confectioner, radar operator, Fishery Officer and lorry driver. Now, in his fifty-sixth year, Leonard unwittingly embarked upon the fifth and most remarkable phase of his life: as an inventor.

CHAPTER SEVEN

ALL CRAFTSMEN SHARE A KNOWLEDGE

ONE evening in September 1968, Leonard drove back from the Nurseries to the cottage, had a cup of tea and a slice of bread, and went out. He was gone for three hours. Hazel saw that the car was outside, so that he could not have gone far. She strolled past Len Curry's cottage and saw a light coming from the barn nearby.

'Len! Are you there?'

The barn door was partly open. Hazel peered inside: a single naked light bulb illuminated part of the abandoned barn. Leonard, in shirt sleeves, was sawing at a piece of metal on an improvised work-bench made from one of the orange boxes Hazel had first brought to the cottage.

'What are you doing?'

Leonard looked up at her and grinned. 'Welcome to the workshop,' he said.

Beside him lay the torn cigarette packet with his first crude thoughts on Andy's artificial legs. Close to it was a much larger, more detailed working diagram, half-covered with Leonard's small, almost incomprehensible writing.

'Oh Len – what's the good? They'll never accept anything you suggest. They have specialists down at Chailey who do nothing else but make up things for children like Andy. Anyway, where'd you get the gear?'

It appeared that Leonard had discussed his problems with a colleague at the Nurseries. The colleague had friends who belonged to the Huntingdon Round Table. The members had had a whip-round for what they thought might be useful articles for Leonard. With wry pride, Leonard showed Hazel his treasures: a hacksaw with two spare blades, a couple of files, some lengths of wood, a long chromium-plated rod, and the contents of a wrecked washing-machine that Leonard had discovered and cannibalized.

'If Andy came into this barn now – with his artificial legs on – it would take him about half an hour to move from the door to that wall over there. So long as Chailey insists that he wears them down there, I'm going to see if I can't make walking a bit easier and a bit faster for him.'

In spare moments from September to December 1968, Leonard worked at his new design. Nights, weekends, early mornings he began to spend in the barn, and Hazel grew intolerably lonely. There was no radio or television set in the cottage – any spare cash went into buying parts for 'Andy's gadget'. But both of them realized what this preoccupation of Leonard's meant. They would have to bring Andy back for Christmas with them in order to be able to try out Leonard's system.

They were due to pick Andy up on the Saturday morning. Leonard spent from seven on the Friday evening until four o'clock the following morning, working to finish his gadget before motoring down to Chailey. He rolled into bed exhausted. He had done all he could without the artificial limbs to work with. Once again, despite all their worries, both Leonard and Hazel found the journey to Chailey exhilarating. They could deny it no longer: they were positively eager to see Andy again. But again when they first met him, and for more than an hour afterwards, Andy was reserved and tight, deriving, apparently, no enjoyment from their presence, or the prospect of a Christmas spent away from Chailey. As before, however, by the time the journey was completed, he was relaxed and chattering, and bouncing with eagerness to see Leonard's gadget in practice.

That night, when Andy was asleep, Leonard took the entire structure of arms, bucket seat, harness and legs into his workshop, and began assimilating into it his own modifications. The existing movement allowed Andy to move his false feet not more than half an inch at a time. Leonard estimated that his device would enable the child to have a stride of at least four, and possibly six, inches. The ankles were articulated in rubber bushes, and the feet kept track side by side by means of a tie-rod. When Andy was fully in harness he would rock his bucket-seat. The movement would operate a cam on a spindle, which would turn the feet and propel them forward. For extra manoeuvrability, Andy could move in any direction by pressing a tiny lever with his own foot. This would release the tie-rod, and he would be able to turn round.

That morning, before entrusting Andy to the new device, Hazel washed him and weighed him. She compared his weight now with what it had been when he had left them in the summer, and found that he had lost weight in the intervening months. This was something she would have to think out carefully. But Andy was impatient to try his new gadget, so Leonard strapped him into his artificial limbs, and explained to him, step by step, what he had to do in order to move. Andy followed the instructions immediately, wriggled his buttocks, rocked from side to side, and fairly bounded across the room. The speed of his movement astonished even Leonard, and Hazel had to run forward to prevent Andy from cannoning into the wall. Andy was excited, and a little afraid of this new power. Leonard was merely afraid. For Andy to fall over when the artificial legs were static would be highly dangerous: to fall over when he was moving at speed would be almost certainly fatal. Leonard removed his device, took it outside, and smashed it to pieces with a hammer. There would have to be some other way to get Andy moving faster, but without danger.

Meantime, Hazel was giving thought to the matter of Andy's weight: why should he be losing at Chailey the weight he put on at Nursery Cottages? Simple observation of the boy's eating habits confirmed her suspicions. He was accustomed to eating with his gas-powered artificial arms. These ended in two prongs. Into these his spoon would be inserted by whoever was supervising the meal. It was then Andy's problem to get food on to the long spoon, and raise it to his mouth. In order to make the right angle for the naturally jerky movement of the spoon, Andy would have to lean hard backwards, and much of the food never reached his mouth at all. In time, the boy became so bored with seeing food splatter everywhere but in the right place that he would make do with less than his body required. The moment Hazel or Leonard suggested feeding him themselves, he would eat far more, and with far more enjoyment. But all three realized that this method would have to be abandoned once Leonard could come up with some device that would enable Andy to eat heartily – and unaided. This was something else for him to consider, along with a safer, faster means of transport for the boy.

When Leonard and Hazel returned Andy to Chailey after the Christmas holidays, Leonard asked to see the equipment they had at the hospital which gave the disabled children mobility. Chailey showed him a machine they knew as 'Emma'. A child in artificial legs would move straight from the floor to a platform on Emma which, in first position, was at floor level. The child would back on to the platform, lower a safety bar, then, by operating a switch, lift the platform from ground level to a little over two inches above the ground. Now they could drive the machine in any direction, and get about the hospital faster and more safely than by hobbling on their artificial legs. Leonard studied Emma for a long time, then asked:

'If this takes a child from A to B – what does he do, what can he do, when he reaches B?'

To the Chailey authorities the question seemed irrelevant. Leonard explained what he was getting at to Hazel, on the way home.

'Look,' he said, 'a child on Emma can reach a particular place, provided he has a smooth surface to travel on. But having got there, he has to step out of Emma and do whatever he wants to do in those confounded limbs. What I want to do is to devise a machine in which Andy can travel without the artificial limbs altogether, but capable of allowing him to achieve something at the other end – with his own physical capabilities – and without leaving the machine at all!'

'But even if you think of something,' Hazel pointed out, 'and you think you can make it work, how much is it going to cost? That Emma machine was worth about £600 at least – and where do we find that kind of money? You'll have to be reasonable, Len.'

Since his accident in the lorry, Len had been laid up for

almost two and a half years. Now, after being back at work for a year, he was still in debt, and his basic wage of £14 10s a week gave them no margin for expensive engineering experiments.

'I'll just have to see what I can scrounge,' he said. That night he went to the workshop and began thinking on paper.

Seven hours later he had come up with a sketch for a vehicle. It would be a small, low three-wheeler. Andy would sit in a seat between the front wheels, and these would also be the driving wheels. That would be the start. Leonard began asking around, going to junk shops and scrap-metal dealers. Having learned the reason for Leonard's requests, most individuals and some firms were only too happy to give Leonard fragments of raw materials. He decided, early on, that the cheapest and lightest material for the bodywork of the car would be glass-fibre. This he obtained. Carting his job lot of metals and machinery into the workshop, he began to translate his sketch into reality. Len Curry, their neighbour, offered to do all the necessary welding on the car, and this was to be a major relief to Leonard. Now he had to think about powering the vehicle.

A boy with no arms cannot steer a wheel. Power and movement must therefore be completely re-thought. Andy would have to use his shoulders to direct the machine, so that steering could be controlled by shoulder-pads on each side of his seat. But Andy had flippers, and his left flipper was sufficiently prehensile now – thanks largely to Hazel's efforts – to be of use to the little driver. So, thought Leonard, his shoulders will control movement to right and left, and his flipper will control forward and reverse movement.

The concept seemed simple – it was simple at this stage – but it was a staggering breakthrough. If a tiny, armless child with only the rudiments of legs could drive a car, what else might he be able to accomplish, given the time and the ingenuity?

During the early months of 1969 Leonard continued to beseech, cajole and scrounge. Eventually, he had all the parts he needed – in principle; now he could set up the mechanical and electrical systems to power the car.

Andy came to the Nursery Cottages in May for a holiday,

jabbering with excitement about his new car. Although they did not reach home until almost midnight, the child was all for leaping into the car that moment.

The following morning Hazel carried Andy down to the kitchen: there was his own car: a white, glass-fibre body, and a little cockpit with some very interesting instruments ranged round the side. Leonard explained slowly and carefully, as always, how the machine would work. Andy, fascinated, took it all in. The driving-motor was a 12-volt car dynamo which drove a differential through a worm-drive. Steering was to be done by braking. When Andy pressed his left shoulder-pad, the left wheel would begin to lock, and the right wheel, still continuing to move freely, would begin to describe an arc. The reverse would be true of the right shoulder-pad. To make the car go forwards or backwards, Andy would use his flipper to push a small lever which in turn controlled a variable resistance.

'Yes, yes,' the boy was saying. 'Can I go now, Daddy?' He went.

From the house to the end of the lane, forwards and backwards, spinning and turning, fast and slow. Within ten minutes Andy was manipulating his machine like an expert. Hazel shed a few quiet tears, and Leonard, smoking hard, began to note down such modifications as might be necessary. The boy was jubilant, and had no wish to leave the car even for roast beef and Yorkshire pudding. As Hazel lifted him out of the cockpit, Leonard snapped his fingers.

'That's it!' he said, and strode off briskly towards the workshop.

Over lunch, he told Hazel and Andy what was on his mind:

'At the moment, if Andy wants to go driving, we have to carry him to the car and put him in it. Then he has freedom of movement. But when he wants to get out again, we have to lift him out. So he's not really free at all, is he?'

'So what're you going to do?' said Hazel incredulously. 'Build a little crane he can operate himself?'

'I may do,' said Leonard. 'It may have to come to that.'

Leonard went to the barn and began roughing out a sketch, assessing costs and practicability. He did not see how he could do it, yet he knew he had to. He had faith in his own technical ability, and now he needed to extend that ability and his own ingenuity to lengths he had never imagined feasible.

They drove Andy back to Chailey, and promised that he would be able to come to the cottage for the long summer holidays. By now Andy had no doubt in his mind that they meant what they said. It was late by the time he had been undressed, washed. and carried to his ward. The nurse put him to bed, wished him good night, and went out.

As they drove home that night Leonard and Hazel once again made a few financial calculations. They were heavily in debt at the bank – Andy's car had cost much more than Leonard had hoped – and with only his small wage coming in weekly, they could see no hopes of whittling away at the overdraft or of collecting sufficient money to advance the work on a new vehicle for Andy.

'It's going to be a long, hard summer,' said Leonard.

'Aren't they all?'

But they had, perhaps unconsciously, cleared the most massive hurdle of all. Now, the prospect of life without Andy was unthinkable. Their task over the next few years would be to provide the child with a permanent home, and to give him freedom.

Leonard stopped the car and fumbled for a cigarette. His wife said nothing: she recognized the symptoms. Leonard inhaled deeply, and ran his fingers through his hair, then looked out of the window, thinking. He sighed, and glanced at Hazel.

'The thing is,' he said, 'that we need Andy as much as he needs us.'

CHAPTER EIGHT

ANDY CHANGES HIS NAME

DURING the period beginning January 1969, when Leonard was to find his most fruitful phase of inventiveness, another major effort was being made: Leonard and Hazel decided to adopt Andy. They themselves were unable to pin-point one particular day on which they decided 'Andy must be ours'; what is certain is that sometime in 1968 they had approached Andy's natural mother and asked her permission to apply to adopt the boy. The mother consented. Leonard began to make enquiries. Then the mother, fearful perhaps of publicity, abruptly withdrew her consent. Leonard and Hazel were astonished and dismayed, but, according to the law, could take no further steps in the matter. Fortunately, because of the publicity given locally to Leonard's remarkable inventions, Andy's natural mother came to realize that Andy's best hopes of achieving some sort of independence lay with the Wileses. In February 1970 Leonard and Hazel met Andy's mother and her husband, in a final effort to win a change of heart over the matter.

At the beginning of 1969, Hazel had begun to keep a full diary of the events in their lives. Situated where they were, in the remote cottage in Huntingdonshire, a long way from neighbours or friends, most of the time without television and much of it without radio, Hazel was bound to feel lonely. Leonard's driving took him away from home a good deal, and when he was at home he spent all his spare time in the barn, working on devices for Andy. So Hazel, by nature gregarious, began to pour out her feelings on to the pages of her diaries. By any standards they form a fascinating and detailed account of the daily hopes and fears, the endless frustrations, the continuous battle against poverty and bankruptcy; but that they should have been written by a woman who was not literate until she was in her late teens is altogether remarkable.

> *20th February, 1970:* We met Andy's Parents today they have said we can have Andy at last his mother realizes what we are trying to do for him. I am sure she will not change her mind again. I do wish we could tell Andy what is going on but I think it is best to wait until we see him again.

The consent finally obtained, Leonard and Hazel went down to Chailey to discuss the whole matter of Andy's future with Dr. Quibell, Principal of the Hospital, and with the Chief Welfare Officer there.

Leonard showed Dr. Quibell the document signed by Andy's mother which gave Leonard and Hazel authority to act for him in the matter of operations. Leonard soft-pedalled his hopes of adoption, and entered into a discussion concerning ways and means of Andy's living nearer the cottage than he was at present. Each visit involved Leonard and Hazel in a round trip of well over 200 miles. This was expensive and tiring, and cut down the time they could spend with Andy once they arrived at Chailey. Dr. Quibell pointed out that no familiar hospital existed between Chailey and Thrapston. Leonard then contemplated finding a job somewhere in southern Surrey. On their return home he began to make enquiries. But to find reasonable accommodation and employment for them both seemed impossible. Leonard decided the only way out of the situation would be to move forward with their adoption claim as fast as the law would allow, when he could, with more likelihood of success, test his determination to have Andy living with them permanently.

Leonard's solicitor, Robin Boyes of Huntingdon, began the adoption claims with efficiency and despatch. Before long Leonard had seen to it that local and national newspapers were aware of his hopes. There were articles, and a mention on national television. Letters from well-wishers began to arrive; but at the same time Chailey made it plain that they would not be prepared to accept Andy's permanent removal from the hospital.

28th February, 1970: It seems that all at once everyone loves our Andy and yet not one of them wants to give him a real home life they all seem to think that he would be better off at Chailey but we know best.

Chailey claimed that Andy needed constant medical attention. Leonard pointed out that during the long holidays with them he had not needed to see a doctor once; that he was, apart from his limb deficiencies, a perfectly healthy and normal child. Chailey remained unconvinced.

Part of the pattern of adoption procedure is to produce a full medical report on the prospective parents-to-be, as well as on the child. In Hazel's diary an entry occurs whose irony was later to mock her constantly.

3rd April, 1970: Took Andy to Peterborough, the doctor signed the papers to say we were O.K. and did not charge us the usual fee had a good talk to Andy about adoption and explain to him he really is part of us now.

The local Medical Officer of Health was satisfied as to the Wileses' physical fitness, and wrote to Chailey asking for a full report on Andy's condition. A month went by, and he wrote again. Meantime, Hazel and Leonard were becoming involved with efforts to obtain compensation for children affected by thalidomide, and to this end went to London to a meeting of parents. Lady Hoare, a prime mover in the initial campaign to raise funds for the children, presided at the meeting. Hazel's diary entry describes their situation:

2nd May, 1970: Got to London at Noon the meeting had started Lady Hoare said we are not parents I got very cross and left meeting, a man came up and gave me £1 and said he would help us.

Over three months went by, and still Chailey had not forwarded a medical report on Andy to the Huntingdonshire Health Offices. Until this arrived, nothing could be done to further adoption proceedings. Hazel, meantime, recognizing that sooner or later there would be some investigation into her and Leonard's marital background, was becoming increasingly depressed:

> *12th July, 1970:* . . . the vicar did not call yesterday I do not know why it seems to me no one wants to come and see us anymore, I still do not think they will let me adopt Andy because of my past I only wish that my life had been different . . .

Five months had now passed without any communication from Chailey. One evening the Assistant Medical Officer of Health called on Leonard. She was sympathetic to their situation, and asked Leonard if he could think of any way of obtaining the necessary report from Chailey, since official channels had apparently failed. Leonard, normally the gentlest of men, said he could think of a way. He asked the Assistant Officer to let Chailey know that unless the report was forthcoming within the week, he would take the story and all relevant correspondence to every major newspaper in the country. Seven days later:

> *21st August, 1970:* Got medical report at last why do people have to be so bloody-minded now the adoption can go ahead.

The months of tension were wearing them all down. Andy cried bitterly whenever he had to return to Chailey; Hazel became more despondent about their chances; and Leonard wondered why nothing legal could ever happen on time. However, in September their solicitor informed them that the court hearing would take place at 10.15 a.m. on Thursday, 5th November. 'Don't think it's possible,' Hazel noted in her diary. Her gloom was justified. Legal machinery had forgotten to obtain a Probation Officer's report as to the social and psychological suitability of Leonard and Hazel for the role of adoptive parents. The hearing was adjourned until 7th January. The probing was about to begin.

Miss Hewitt, the local Probation Officer, paid a number of visits to Leonard and Hazel. Her task was unenviable, and the paper evidence against the Wiles couple was very weighty. Hazel had had three previous marriages, two of which had ended in divorce; both her children had been removed from her care and protection. Leonard had had one previous marriage, ending in divorce; he and Hazel had technically lived in adultery for several years before they were able to marry. Leonard was now almost sixty – an advanced age for any man wishing to become father to a small boy. Against this Miss Hewitt had to set the remarkable progress Hazel and Leonard were making with Andy, and the love that was evidently illuminating all their lives.

> *7th December, 1970:* Im fed up a woman came to see us about the adoption I don't think we shall get him my past is against me She was here two hours and seemed very nice I do love Andy so much and so does Len I have not been a very nice person.

Miss Hewitt had to be practical, and a further visit did nothing to lift the depression that had now settled on Hazel and Leonard; did little to encourage a merry Christmas or thoughts of a happy New Year. The unbearable tension Hazel was experiencing is reflected in a note she wrote early on New Year's Day, 1971:

> If I have to give up Andy I shall go away and never come back it would be impossible to stay after being with him so long and loving him as I do. I did not mean to become his adopted mother it just came out that way he has become part of me, he is a wonderful boy and he loves me as well and that makes me very proud.

Two days before the hearing, Leonard's solicitor called at the cottage. His news was not reassuring. Having looked into the troubled past of both Hazel and Leonard, Miss Hewitt had reluctantly decided that she would, in all professional honesty, have to oppose their claims to adoption before the judge on 7th January. Hazel wept, and Leonard became unusually bitter.

'It amazes me,' he told Mr. Boyes, 'that the Welfare people should choose as advisers on adoption women who have had no experience of the ups and downs of married life. How can a spinster – or a bachelor – have any conception at all of the strains and miseries that lead people to get divorced? It's like giving someone who's never driven a car in his life a manual of procedure, then appointing him Chief Driving Examiner! It just doesn't make sense!'

Mr. Boyes attempted to explain the way the law must operate, but Hazel and Leonard were too distressed to accept a dispassionate view.

'It's taken two years!' said Leonard. 'This whole wretched business has taken two years, and when we thought we had everything going for us at last, we're shot down in flames.'

Andy, of course, had been informed stage by stage of the progress of the adoption claim, and he was required to be in court with Leonard and Hazel when the case was judged.

They reached the Town Hall in Huntingdon long before the hearing was due. Mr. Boyes was there to meet them, and he advised them on court procedure, tactfully pointing out that no matter what the pressures or provocations, they must not themselves attempt to play Defence Counsel. Their case was second to be heard. Andy was sitting on Hazel's lap, and Hazel gripped Leonard's hand tightly as their names were called and the judge bent over to examine his papers. He looked up gravely.

'I have examined all the documents in this case. Mr. and Mrs. Leonard Wiles appear to me the most suitable people to have this child, and I have no hesitation in signing the adoption order.' And that was it. Less than ninety seconds decided what had taken over two years to reach the court.

Outside Hazel could not believe their good fortune. An entry in her diary vividly recalls the moment:

I was so surprised I just cried. The Judge said it was quite clear we were right for Terry. When we got out I kissed Mr. Boyes even Miss Hewitt she never said very much to us. Len bought me some new scissors for dressmaking I did nothing at home, too excited,

But there was one final incident before the new family left Huntingdon. As Hazel walked down the High Street carrying Andy in her arms he was shouting, 'I'm adopted! I'm adopted!' Passers-by paused and stared in amazement. Here was a woman carrying what appeared to be a babe in arms; yet the babe, in the most powerful of voices, was proclaiming to the world his delight at being adopted. Andy was now nearly nine years old, and he was determined that on his birthday five days later he would have shed all traces of his former identity. Hazel and Leonard had told him that, when his surname was altered to Wiles, he could also change his Christian name. Andy willingly grasped his chance of total escape from a past he had come to detest so bitterly, and when Leonard took him to the County Court offices to register the change of name, it was Andy who informed the clerk that he did not wish to be Andrew Wiles.

'I see, son. What do you want to be called?'

'Terrence. Terrence with two r's. Write it down, please, will you?'

The clerk obliged, and Andy became Terrence Wiles. From that moment on he would refuse to acknowledge any name other than Terrence or Terry; and this refusal was to bring him for a time into conflict with the authorities at Chailey. The day following his birthday he was due to return to the Hospital. It was to be the task of Leonard and Hazel in the months ahead to make it possible for their son to live permanently at home with them. For the time being at least they must accept the authority of Chailey.

CHAPTER NINE

NO COAL, NO GAS, NO ELECTRIC

WHILST Leonard and Hazel were fighting to call Terry their own son, there was another infinitely more protracted, infinitely more humiliating campaign to be waged – against poverty and bankruptcy.

Hazel's diary makes bitter reading. So long as she was on her own, with no Terry to look after, she had too much time to consider the inadequacies of her household. Leonard, busy and driving by day, and in the workshop at night, was able to cut himself off from financial worries for the greater part of his waking hours. He needed to. Only ruthless single-mindedness was going to turn his ideas for Terry's next car into a reality. But Hazel had all the time in the world – despite her constant search for work – to brood on lack of money; to face the bailiffs and tradesmen; to answer the increasingly severe letters from shopkeepers. Everything that was not vital to keeping them fed and in the cottage went into the workshop. The strain became appalling.

Frequently Hazel sat in the cottage without heat or light or radio. Leonard worked in the freezing outbuilding where, fortunately, there was a separate electricity meter. Leonard was conscious that his employer was generously forgetting to ask him to pay the bill for the electricity he was using in the workshop; in return Leonard refused to use any form of heating. He would work, sometimes through the night, with fog or snow drifting into the barn. Sometimes his hands became so cold and numb that he would have to go into Len Curry's cottage and restore the circulation under the hot water tap. He was approaching sixty, he had had two massive accidents and was no longer strong. But his belief in what he was doing sustained him, as it sustained Hazel, despite her greater vulnerability.

Leonard was determined that the second car, which he had already christened the 'Bomb', would be one into which, and from which, the boy could move without any assistance. He had certainly toyed with the idea of some form of crane, to be suspended over the car seat, but soon abandoned this as absurdly expensive and static. No, Terry must be able to get into the Bomb on his own. Leonard tried and rejected a number of notions, and after a month or two was no nearer the ideal solution. Until one morning he went out to the car and opened the boot to fetch out some kindling for the cottage fire.

His eyes fell on the car jack. He picked it up, forgot about the kindling, and set the jack down on the lane. If this small mechanism, he thought, is capable of lifting a full-sized car, then it's capable of lifting a small boy like Terry. From then on his car went without its jack.

Leonard put a pulley on the top of the jack, where the screw handle is normally found, attached the pulley to a motor – there was the embryonic lift for Terry. Over the next few months Leonard began drafting his plans for the Bomb in fine detail; and went on spending money on raw materials.

13th August, 1969: We are getting short of food....

14th November, 1969: Its getting me down no money all the time I do wish I could get work it would be a great help.

16th November, 1969: Len out in the barn working on Terry's bomb.... Bailiff came this morning for money.

Leonard began discussing his lift problem with a number of qualified engineers, but they did not believe that he could possibly combine a lift mechanism and a driving mechanism – on a small scale – in one and the same vehicle, and showed him chapter and verse to prove it. Undaunted, Leonard visited his neighbour, Len Curry. This Leonard, by trade a motor mechanic, had a well-equipped workshop. He listened to Leonard's ideas and agreed to help him. He, too, was an entirely self-taught engineer. Leonard began to feel that at last he was making some progress.

After four months, Leonard was ready to try out the lifting mechanism with Terry. They found that it would raise the boy nine inches from ground level without difficulty. Now Leonard had to incorporate this device into the body of the Bomb. Fortunately, Leonard was working with practical assistance from other quarters. He showed his sketches for the proposed bodywork of the vehicle to Bob Robinson of Arch Motors in Huntingdon. Bob Robinson was a highly experienced frame-maker and had worked on many of the country's leading racing cars. He saw a practicality in Leonard's sketches which appealed to him. With his firm's blessing he offered to make up the frame to Leonard's specifications if Leonard would cut the metal into the shapes he had designed.

This was a colossal step forward. Leonard managed somehow to find the tools to cut the metal, and he delivered the sections to Bob Robinson, together with his detailed plans for the bodywork. While Arch Motors began assembling the strange kit, Leonard could now concentrate on the driving mechanism.

In all, from conception to final delivery the Bomb had taken over a year to evolve, and the inroads into Leonard's bank balance had been terrifying. Yet when Terry came home to try out the Bomb for the first time, neither Leonard nor Hazel had any thoughts except for the tiny child who now sat impatiently in the kitchen, looking with awe and delight at this strange new device.

'There it is, Terry!' said Leonard. 'All you have to do is get in and drive.'

Terry, fairly beaming, scuttled across the kitchen floor on his bottom and scrambled on to the seat. His face glowed with amazement and delight.

'It works! It works, Dad!'

The local newspaper heard about the Bomb and wanted to do a story with photographs. A few days later BBC's *Tomorrow's World* asked if they might make a short film about Terry and Leonard's invention. Leonard and Hazel needed time to think about it. They were both aware of the positive side of publicity: interest bred sympathy, and sympathy might bring in much-needed money to further Leonard's inventions. On the other hand, what would publicity do to or for Terry? Would he want to be seen as a freak and an abnormality? They discussed the matter with the boy. He had no hesitations when once they had told him what publicity might achieve.

'Sooner or later,' they told him 'you've got to live your life with normal people, all the time. And when they first meet you they're going to stare, because you are quite different from anything most of them have ever seen in their lives. But if you want the life any boy of your age wants, you'll have to mix. You'll have to get used to curiosity.'

A child less forceful and resilient than Terry might have objected – and understandably. But Terry had placed his future in Leonard's and Hazel's hands.

'If you think it's right,' he said, 'let's go ahead.'

The *Tomorrow's World* team made their short film, and after a number of delays it went out. By then Terry was back at Chailey; Hazel, without a television set, was with friends; and Leonard was at Preston, half-way through a long lorry haul. The amount of genuine interest was impressive – but the Wileses were again short of money.

They had agreed to visit Terry one weekend. They had borrowed a vehicle for that purpose and, by eating very little throughout the week, they calculated that they had just enough money for petrol to get them to Chailey and back. But they had promised the child this visit. They breakfasted on two cups of tea, shared their last cigarette, and went across the lane to the borrowed car. Just then the postman appeared, and called to them.

'Forget it,' said Leonard, starting the car, 'it can only be a bill.'

'Let's just see, anyway,' said Hazel.

The one letter was from an old-age pensioner. She had anonymously sent them a five-pound note. That day they took Terry for chicken and chips in a basket, and invested in twenty cigarettes.

Len returned to his workshop. He wanted to work on an idea

he had had – a mobile lift. Hazel's diary records the progress of another lean winter:

> *28th January, 1970:* Len has been up since 2.30 a.m. working in the barn went off to work at 8 a.m. with no breakfast.
>
> *15th February, 1970:* Len in barn till 2 a.m. No coal, no gas, no electric

Occasionally, just occasionally, there were lighter moments:

> *19th February, 1970:* Len is funny, he bought me a box of Milk Tray today, he called me outside and climbed onto his Lorry and jumped off gave me them saying The Lady Loves Milk Tray just like the TV adverts, it was so funny I did laugh I don't know where he gets all the energy. . . .

In March Terry came home for Easter – at this time the adoption was in its early stages – and there were two significant events for Hazel to record. Up to this time Terry, used to sleeping in a protective cradle at Chailey, could not adapt to a normal bed in the cottage. He was anxious, restless and constantly troubled by nightmares. Now, with the prospect of adoption to hang on to, he began to have easier nights and his nightmares became less frequent.

It was also during this Easter holiday that the eating breakthrough occurred. Once again Hazel had weighed Terry on his return from Chailey and she found that during the term there he had lost seven ounces, a considerable amount for a boy of his tiny stature. Leonard set aside other things and concentrated on designing an aid which would enable Terry to feed himself without the use of artificial arms. One day, Hazel had produced sausages and mash, one of Terry's favourites. To make sure that he enjoyed it fully, she began feeding him with a spoon, as one would a baby. Terry ate for a while with evident pleasure, then asked suddenly:

'Can I have a big spoon, please? I want to try something.' Always anxious to let him help himself where feasible, Hazel brought him a serving spoon. Leonard was fascinated and excited. This was precisely the kind of relationship he was working to encourage – a mutual constructiveness. They watched the boy carefully. Terry took the end of the handle of the spoon in his mouth, and succeeded in scooping on to it a lump of sausage. Then he carefully set the spoon down on the edge of his plate, with much of the handle projecting, and slowly eased it round with his shoulder until the mouth-piece of the spoon was now close to the plate's rim. Then he bent forward and took the piece of sausage with his mouth.

'It's ridiculous,' said Leonard. 'I've been racking my brains over this self-feeding business for two years, and now here's Terry giving me the answer in twenty seconds.'

Instantly he disappeared from the table into his workshop. Hazel and Terry burst into laughter and shared the rest of Leonard's meal between them.

That afternoon Leonard came up with a simple gadget that would give Terry complete control of his own eating. No more heaving about with gas-powered arms; no more being fed by Hazel and Leonard in turn. First he hammered out a metal base, large enough to accept any normal dish or plate. To this he attached a vertical clamp, so that the whole device could be carried around, and fixed to any table at which Terry sat. The top of the clamp, a metal spindle, capable of rotating through 360 degrees, was high enough above the base for Terry to be able to reach it without leaning any distance. To the spindle Leonard welded a short horizontal arm, with two tiny finger-like projections. Into this the handle of the spoon would fit exactly, and stay firm. Five hours' work and the rough prototype was ready. Leonard tested it a dozen times in the workshop. He could see no evident flaw. But it was Terry who would have to manipulate it.

Hazel provided fish and chips for the evening meal. With some ceremony Leonard fixed his gadget to the table, put Terry's meal in front of him, set the spoon in the projection, and said:

'Away you go, Terry.'

There was no need for explanations. Terry removed the spoon from the spindle in his teeth, scooped up a couple of chips, returned the spoon to the metal fingers, then swivelled the spindle round 90 degrees with his shoulder. The spoon, with the chips on it, was directly in front of him, at mouth level, and only inches away. Terry helped himself. Hazel and Leonard left their food untouched as the small boy delved into his meal. Towards the end, when he had a spoonful of fish ready to eat, Terry observed excitedly, 'Daddy, I can help feed the others when I go back, can't I? Look – you have this bit.'

Leonard rose, mumbled something, and went outside. For the first time in his association with Terry he was moved to tears. Here was an almost impossibly damaged child, for whom every ordinary activity in life would be a constant struggle, already concerned to help others like himself.

'Come on, Daddy, or we'll be eating your supper as well!'

21st March, 1970: Up at 8 a.m. Terry slept well it is wonderful to see him eating without any help.

But so many achievements seemed balanced by a setback.

17th April, 1970: Terry back to Chailey he wanted to be held all the way.

Leonard took his feeding device to Chailey and demonstrated its use to the staff. They nodded and commented on how interesting it was, and Leonard left. Shortly afterwards he discovered that Terry was not allowed to use it at Chailey. He telephoned to find out why. He was told that Terry was accustomed to using his false arms by now, and he would find the change-over to the new device distracting. Leonard told them that when the child was with them at the cottage, he ate well and put on weight – weight which was lost during the term at Chailey. He was informed that Terry would continue to use his artificial limbs.

'Until we get him home with us for good,' an exasperated Leonard told Hazel, 'all the progress he makes here will go for nothing.' He went back to the workshop and switched on the drill.

Not long after this came another setback – from their point of view a very alarming one. While transferring a load from the lorry to a customer, Leonard strained his back so severely that he was obliged to go home. There began a period of intense pain, and even less money.

> *9th November, 1970:* Bailiff came for money today we hadnt got any he was very good and gave us an extra week.

At the end of the year Hazel reflected on the situation as she saw it:

> Im trying very hard not to lose faith, my darling Len trys so much to help other people but no one wants to know, I cannot say how much he has spent trying to make life easy for our Terry, he wants to help other children as well but no one will help him. I try very hard not to get bitter, but when you see everyone else getting on and we stay poor it really takes a lot not to get bitter at times.

Shortly after this the family were involved in another struggle. By now Terry was legally the adopted son of Leonard and Hazel but, in accordance with instructions from Chailey, the boy was still to spend his boyhood there, during term-time. Anxious not to cause trouble after all the problems they had had to adopt Terry, Leonard and Hazel dutifully complied. After Christmas, the boy had been returned to Chailey. On Friday 5th March, Leonard was driving not far from the hospital, and decided to bring Terry home for a weekend. What he saw enraged him beyond measure. The child was frightened and exhausted. Leonard questioned him. Terry came up with an extraordinary story of having been held down whilst a doctor stuck needles into him. Leonard wished to establish how much of the story was childish melodrama and how much was truth. He went to the Administrative Office, where there was a final showdown.

It appeared that the Chailey doctors, rightly worried about Terry's size, had decided to run some blood tests on him, with a view to putting him on some medical regime which might encourage his growth.

'But how on earth do you take blood samples from a boy

with no arms and effectively no legs?' Leonard wanted to know. 'And why, when you knew this was going to take place, did you not first consult me? I am his adoptive father, and without my consent you have no authority to so much as break his skin.'

The explanations were not satisfactory to Leonard. He left with Terry in his arms, and motored to London in the old van. En route, the water pump seized up. Leonard fiddled and juggled, and the van started again. By now Leonard was very tired, and anxious to get home quickly. As a result he negotiated the roundabout at the Elephant and Castle a little too enthusiastically, and soon there was a police patrol car flagging him down. The policeman sternly cautioned Leonard and took out his notebook. Then he caught sight of Terry's one bright little eye fixed on him. The constable unbent. Leonard told a tale of a country bumpkin in the big city for the first time, unsure of his way and frightened of the traffic. The constable cautioned him gently, and Leonard drove on.

As he crossed Seven Sisters Road half the exhaust system fell off. Leonard had to stop the van and collect the various remnants. Having made some running repairs with pieces of wire, Leonard again drove off.

As the van approached Biggleswade he noticed what appeared to be a two-mile crocodile of traffic. Leonard moved over, and sped forward driving in the crown of the road, passing immobile cars and lorries. Abruptly a police patrol car eased out of the jam and began following him. He was coaxed into a layby. The driver and his companion began a close examination of the van, and kept up a running commentary on its defects.

'Are you aware that you have been driving dangerously?' they said, 'and that your vehicle is unfit to be on the road?' A notebook was produced, and Leonard believed that his days of lorry-driving would shortly be curtailed.

'What're you bothering my Dad for?' piped Terry.

'Who said that?' asked one constable, playing his torch around the cabin. He saw the twenty-one-inch boy looking at him vengefully.

'He yours, mate?'

'Yes. He's unwell, and I was anxious to get him to bed.'

The constable scratched his head. 'Hop it, and don't take any more risks. But if the local bobbies catch you in that van you'll be for it.'

Leonard thanked them warmly, and drove off. As they approached Brampton the van began to sneeze and steam and protest. It slowed down to a crawl, and Leonard just managed to coax it down the lane to the cottage, then it gave out completely and finally. Leonard carried Terry into the cottage, where Hazel washed him and put him to bed. That night, interrupted by Terry's nightmares, Hazel and Leonard again took stock.

They now had no transport, no money, and a fight with Chailey on their hands.

'It can't get any worse, Len, it really can't.'

'I hope not,' said Leonard.

But it could. Much worse.

CHAPTER TEN

THE LONG, HARD SUMMER

THE first and most important task, in Leonard's and Hazel's eyes, was to ensure that Terry would never again return to Chailey. Leonard had arrived home with the boy late on Friday night. At ten the following morning he telephoned to Chailey and told them he would not be bringing Terry back again. On Monday he contacted the Education Department of the Huntingdonshire County Council and gave them the same information. He had expected sympathy and reassurance. In the event he was told that unless he took Terry back to Chailey immediately there would be a great deal of trouble. They had already paid Chailey the child's fees for the term, in advance. Leonard repeated his assurance: the boy would never go back to Chailey.

Within a few days he received a letter from the Huntingdonshire County Council, asking him to go down to Chailey and discuss the whole matter with Dr. Quibell, the Principal. The Council would pay his expenses. Leonard readily agreed, and the following day, in a borrowed vehicle, he drove down to Sussex.

The meeting was not a success. Dr. Quibell had no wish to be cross-examined, so Leonard rose and made for the door, saying that there was no point in his staying on. He would have to tell the Huntingdonshire County Council that the journey had been a complete waste of time. Dr. Quibell, with Terry's interests in mind, asked Leonard to settle down and talk things over. Things were talked over, in great detail, for an hour and a half. Dr. Quibell felt that Terry would do far better at the school there; he believed that the new Hendon artificial arms would be of immense value to the boy, and he was certain that the highly qualified staff under his control would accomplish far more for Terry than Leonard could with his stunted means. Leonard disagreed over the use of any sort of artificial limbs for the boy, and over Dr. Quibell's proposals to increase his growth-rate.

'We have to accept he's tiny,' said Leonard, 'but that in itself isn't necessarily a complete disadvantage. Other children in his situation are getting too heavy already, and the more they rely on these artificial things, the less chance they'll have to build up what muscles they've got. As to the new Hendon arms – they're clumsy and impracticable.'

Since neither man would give way on what he believed to be essential features of the argument, Leonard left Chailey and returned home. (He learned, about a month later, that the whole Hendon project had been closed down, since progress was felt to be unsatisfactory.) He still had the Huntingdonshire County Council to placate.

Included in his report on the meeting with Dr. Quibell was a formal request for Terry to be admitted to Brampton County Junior School – as a normal pupil. After a week or so he had his reply. It would not be possible for Terry to be educated at a normal school, and he must be returned to Chailey. No explanations were given. Leonard and Hazel requested a meeting with officials of the County Council, and asked that it might take place as soon as possible, since they were anxious that Terry should attend school immediately.

No meeting was called. Instead there came a letter. The reason why Terry would not be able to attend Brampton School was that the medical report from Chailey clearly proved he was incapable of dealing with conditions at a normal school, and that he required constant medical attention. Hazel and Leonard rejected this reason outright, and requested meantime that Terry might be visited by a home tutor until his educational future were decided. This request was refused. Leonard invited members of the County Council to come to see for themselves that Terry was perfectly capable of attending a normal school, and that he required no more medical attention than a normal boy of his age might need.

Five months went by and still Terry was receiving no schooling at all. Leonard wrote to Mrs. Margaret Thatcher at the Department of Education and Science. A senior official came down to the cottage to talk to Leonard, Hazel and Terry. Ultimately a letter came from the Department, citing the Chailey medical report, and advising Leonard to return the boy to Chailey. Infuriated but by no means defeated, Leonard contacted Sir David Renton, the local Member of Parliament, and put the whole case to him. Sir David was sympathetic, and promised to see if Lord Belstead could use his influence and obtain for Terry a trial period at Brampton School. By now the mental strain on Leonard and Hazel was exhausting. But fate, it seemed, was merely marking time before delivering them a number of appalling body-blows.

For months now Leonard had been back in the workshop again, planning a successor to the Bomb. He argued that if the lift he had already made could raise Terry nine inches off the ground, why not develop a more powerful one that could lift him three feet or more? In this way Terry would be able to reach table height and use his flippers as hands. This was going to be Supercar, incorporating all the lessons learned from the Bomb, designed to give Terry greater mobility. Leonard struggled on, working impossible hours, to convert his visions to reality. Supercar must be manoeuvrable. It must be stronger and lighter than the Bomb. Once again Bob Robinson and Arch Motors offered help. They made the tubular frame to Leonard's specifications, while he laboured to work out an improved driving system.

Supercar was proving expensive. In spite of all the gifts he had received, there was no money left. One day a cheque for £250 arrived from the Society for the Aid of Thalidomide Children. Lady Hoare, its founder and driving force, had seen the publicity about Terry, and made this contribution towards Leonard's work. It seemed a tremendous sum of money to them at first, until they did their homework. Leonard set aside £40 which would buy an ancient but sturdy old van, in which they could visit Terry. £60 would pay off some of their local bills; £50 must go towards the development of Supercar; and the rest must go to the bank, whose manager had been extremely patient with Leonard. Within weeks they were again bedevilled with debts. Leonard borrowed more money, privately, dipping crazily into debt to carry on with the work. And as the summer days lengthened, the invention took shape – an engineering marvel within whose tubes and struts was locked every penny they possessed and more beside.

It was an astonishing improvement on the Bomb. When it was almost finished, Terry tried it out with great success and Leonard, with new enthusiasm, took the machine back to the workshop intent on making it even more manoeuvrable. But that meant still more money. And there was another worry.

One evening Leonard came in from work very soberly. He had just learned that the Nurseries by whom he was employed were to be taken over in three weeks' time, and he would be out of work. He did not need to add that since the cottage was tied to the Nurseries, then he and Hazel and Terry would also soon be homeless. Wearily, Leonard composed a letter to the local Council, applying for a council bungalow – preferably one designed for a handicapped person. Hazel, meanwhile, considered her empire.

> It seems to me I do not do too badly. Ive been thinking that means really Thinking. I dont think there are many women who spend a hell of a lot of time chopping wood to make a fire for hot water and making things work out its not that Im forever making do if its no coal its no gas then Im out of food. I dont know how much longer I can go on this way. Soon well have to leave as firm is closing down. I think Ill run away Im not taking the chair and settee Id never live it down they are so dirty and worn.

In mid-August 1971, Leonard's job came to an end, although the new owners of Nursery Cottages had given the Wiles family a few months' grace, and they did not have to move immediately. Leonard decided to take a week from his first redundancy period in which to work on the Supercar. On Monday, 16th August, he rose shortly before four in the morning, made himself a cup of tea, then went to the workshop in the old barn, Sheba at his heels. He had slept little that night, obsessed as he was with removing one or two flaws from the Supercar. The barn was dark and cold but Leonard had become inured to the bleak surroundings. He worked unremittingly until half past six, when he realized he was still very cold. He went back to the kitchen – about fifty yards away – and heated the kettle. While he was there he began making rough plans for a new modification to the Supercar. The water boiled, and Leonard made himself a mug of tea. The tea remained untasted as Leonard became more involved in the plans. Then Sheba began to whine uneasily. Leonard had been in the kitchen for some twenty minutes. He drank the now stale tea and walked out into the lane.

The barn was on fire.

Leonard stood for a moment, stunned and incredulous. Smoke and flames were pouring out of the workshop door, and there were ominous boomings inside. Leonard raced to the nearest telephone and called the Fire Brigade then ran back to the barn with a small fire extinguisher. Hazel, disturbed by the noise and smoke, had by now awoken. She arrived, breathless and appalled, carrying a pail of water. But neither of them could get anywhere near the barn. The walls appeared to be glowing with heat. They heard cans of cellulose paint exploding inside, and the cracking of joists and timbers. Within minutes the entire building was gutted.

They heard the fire engine arrive as in a dream. The local team had lost no time getting there, but the barn was already beyond saving. The flames were extinguished, and after a time Leonard stood with the fire officer in the charred husk of the workshop.

'I hope you're insured, Mr. Wiles,' said the fireman.

'Insured?'

Leonard moved out of the stinking ashes, across the lane and away into a field in front of the cottage. Insurance? When every penny he could lay his hands on had gone directly to the inventions? In that barn lay ruined every tool he had laboriously collected over four years, and every piece of equipment. The two little cars were gone, and the Supercar prototype and the lift seat; an almost-finished dressing machine; a drinking device, wood and tubing and glass-fibre. Something over £2,000 in stock alone, and four years of unstinted labour. Leonard broke down and wept.

Hazel watched, her own heart aching, then crossed the field and joined him.

'Let's have a cup of tea.'

Leonard returned to the cottage like a man in a nightmare, and slumped into a chair. Sheba whined and tried to lick his hands.

'I'm out of work,' he said, after a time. 'Soon we'll have to leave the cottage and we'll have nowhere to live. We're heavily in debt, and how the hell am I going to find another job at my age? – I'm almost sixty! Hazel – how are we going to keep Terry now? Where are we going to keep him?'

Hazel handed him a mug of tea, not trusting herself to answer. If their new predicament were known to the County Council, surely Terry would be removed, willy-nilly, back to Chailey?

Unbelievably, Terry had slept through the fire and the clangour of the fire-engine's arrival. Together, Hazel and Leonard went up to his room and broke the news to him.

The boy listened solemnly and carefully. He was no fool; he knew what this new disaster might mean. He looked at the white, exhausted, well-loved faces of the two people who meant more to him than the whole world, and longed to indulge in the relief of tears. But tears were not wanted now. What could he possibly say to lift their despondency? At last, with rare tact, he made his suggestion.

'There's nothing we can do just now,' he said. 'So let's go fishing.'

Hazel baked a loaf; Leonard discovered that he had left the fishing tackle in a small outhouse: that at least had escaped the fire. So the family went fishing, and unwittingly Terry turned a major disaster into a minor triumph.

He had often accompanied Leonard on fishing trips, and Leonard knew that the child would dearly love to be able to fish on his own. That morning Terry was particularly anxious to keep his father from brooding, so that, when Leonard had made his cast and anchored his rod, the boy said:

'Wish I could have a go, Dad.'

Hazel was about to intervene. She wanted Leonard to try to relax for an hour or two. Then she, too, saw the value of restoring Leonard's mind to activity again.

'Yes, Len,' she said, 'why not let Terry try?'

Leonard began to think. After a while he said:

'Just watch the line for a bit, will you?'

He strode off in the direction of Nursery Cottages.

'Where's Daddy off to?'

'Just you watch the line, Terry. He'll be back.'

Half an hour later Leonard came back with a handful of metal articles in a paper carrier. As Hazel and Terry watched, Leonard made up a support for a smaller fishing rod with some lengths of stout wire. He placed the end of the rod in a metal tube and supported it over the river by means of the cradle he had fashioned. With more wire he fixed the end of the rod to Terry's wheel-chair. Now he had a rod that could be moved from the horizontal to the vertical. He attached a piece of cord about three feet up the rod, and looped the other end round Terry's head. Leonard baited the hook and placed the tackle in the water, then allowed Terry to take over. It seemed impossible that a fish would oblige on cue, but after a few minutes Terry had a bite. He leaned swiftly back in his wheel-chair, the rod rose up, and there was a gudgeon dangling from the end of his line. Terry was in ecstasy. Leonard allowed the boy his triumph, then slipped the fish off the hook and returned it to the river. Hazel and Terry were crowing with delight when Leonard, turning, saw two policemen approaching them.

'Hello, someone's burgled the cottage,' said Terry. When the policemen arrived they were astonished to see the entire Wiles family hysterical with laughter.

They had come, they said, to take a statement from Leonard about the fire. They were most sympathetic, and suggested Leonard should give an interview to the local newspaper about it. Soon, however, they realized that neither Hazel nor Leonard was in any sort of mood to talk to a newspaper. They remained for some time, watching Terry fish, with every evidence of amazement. They went off quietly, muttering together. The following morning the local paper ran a long account of the Wileses' disaster, and by the next post came the gift of £20 in cash from the staff at the newspaper offices. Peterborough Speedway Association heard what had happened, and collected £120 towards new equipment for Leonard. Over the next ten days there were other kindnesses. Twice Leonard was stopped in the street by total strangers. One man give him £5, another £10. Letters came in from readers of the local newspaper, containing £45 from various well-wishers. Others rallied round in a practical manner – soon Leonard had a small but useful set of tools, and a workbench. He could go back into production again – as soon as he had sorted out Terry's schooling.

After a long silence there came a letter from the local authorities, advising Leonard that a doctor from the Huntingdon Health Service would call the following day at 4 p.m. to discuss Terry's education. 'At last,' thought Hazel and Leonard, 'we're making some progress.' The doctor arrived an hour and a half late, and the meeting could not be regarded as satisfactory. She was a stranger to the entire family, and made no attempt to elicit Leonard's reasons for wishing Terry to attend Brampton School. She said the local authorities had found a place for Terry at Hinwick House School – a special school for handicapped boys. Mr. and Mrs. Wiles would have to agree at once, she said, otherwise the place would be lost. Leonard's patience snapped, and there was a stormy scene. The doctor was asked to leave. Afterwards, when they had had time to consider the matter Leonard and Hazel regretted their outburst. They realized the doctor had not known all the facts, and was only doing her duty in recommending Hinwick House. But it was too late for reconciliation now.

Just after the workshop fire, Leonard applied to the Department of Health for a motorized wheel-chair for Terry, so that he would be mobile whatever school he finally went to. The official wheel-chair was a far cry from Supercar, destroyed in the fire. Its seat was fixed, so that Terry would have to be lifted in and out of it. Its manoeuvrability was poor. It moved slowly and only on smooth surfaces. But at least he would be able to taste a little independence.

Leonard expected there would be forms to complete, regulations by which to abide; but he was not prepared for the arrival at the cottage of no fewer than three senior officials:

one from Blackpool, one from Cambridge and one from Oxford. Bewildered, Leonard spoke to them about his own prototypes. The officials talked to Terry for some time, then went away. A few weeks later came a request for Hazel and Leonard to take Terry to Addenbrookes Hospital in Cambridge, where there was a wheel-chair department. Here Terry spent all morning trying out a number of chairs, and it was finally decided that a normal, powered chair with a slightly modified set of controls would be perfectly suitable. The three returned to Brampton and awaited the arrival of the chair.

To their utter surprise a letter arrived asking them to take Terry once more to Addenbrookes, where he would undergo a complete medical examination in order to see if he were physically and mentally capable of driving a powered wheel-chair.

So once again the three travelled to Cambridge, and Terry underwent his examinations. Leonard pointed out, with some exasperation, that barely a week ago the boy had shown himself extremely capable of driving every type of vehicle they possessed, but he was told that the 'driving-test' was one area of responsibility, and the medical examination quite another. They returned to Brampton and once more awaited delivery of the chair.

Several weeks later another official appeared on their doorstep. He had come, he informed them, to inspect the cottage. If the cottage were not suitable for the powered wheel-chair, then Terry would not be given one. By now Leonard and Hazel were beyond surprise or anger. They began to laugh, at first quietly and then uncontrollably. The official, bewildered, failed to observe any grounds for humour. Leonard suggested that if suitability of the cottage were the first criterion, then should not the official gentleman have been the first to see them, rather than the examining gentlemen at Addenbrookes? Finally Leonard told the official that the chair was not for use in the cottage – never had been intended for this purpose – and that the gentleman should pay a visit to Brampton Junior School, which was where they hoped that Terry would be using the chair.

A fortnight went by. A parcel arrived for the Wileses, containing a tray. There was no information with it, and no covering letter. A few days later Leonard telephoned Addenbrookes to ask if Terry's wheel-chair were ready or not. He was told that the wheel-chair was now at St. Albans – had been there for some weeks, in fact, undergoing 'modifications'. Leonard knew that the modifications necessary would have taken any competent mechanic an hour to make so he now rang the engineers at St. Albans.

'Oh, Mr. Wiles,' they said, 'about your son's chair. Yes, It's been ready for some weeks.'

'Then why hasn't it been delivered to us?'

'Well, it's actually short of a part.'

'What part is that?'

'It's a kind of detachable tray.'

'A detachable tray?'

'Yes – a tray you can detach from the chair.'

'But it's here!'

'Where would that be, Mr. Wiles?'

'At home – at the cottage in Brampton.'

'I think you must be mistaken, Mr. Wiles.'

'I am not mistaken. The tray arrived without any sort of advice note some weeks ago. It's in perfectly good condition. What can go wrong with a tray?'

'I see. This is . . . somewhat irregular, you know.'

'I'm sorry. I didn't ask for the tray to be sent here.'

'The manufacturers must have got hold of your address somehow.'

'Yes.'

'Very curious affair, this, Mr. Wiles.'

'Perhaps it is. Can we have the chair now?'

'Oh, we'll deliver it, Mr. Wiles, don't you worry about that.'

'No, thank you. Thank you very much but no. We'll collect it.'

'We normally deliver them from here, you know.'

'I'll collect it. Just tell me where to go and I'll pick it up myself.'

'Well, if you insist.'

'Yes, I do rather.'

In November a caller arrived at the cottage: had Leonard and Hazel heard any more about the matter of Terry's schooling? Leonard told the lady that Sir David Renton intended to achieve something positive when Parliament assembled after the summer recess. But Parliament had by now been long assembled. Leonard promised that if he heard nothing within the week he would take the story to the leading newspapers and let them make of it what they wished, a threat he had issued once before in the battle for Terry's rights. The lady departed. Within two days there arrived a letter from the Huntingdon County Council to say that Terry had been accepted into Brampton County Junior School for a six-month trial period. How long, Leonard wondered, had the letter been lying in the Education Offices before his ultimatum was reported?

So Terry seemed at last free to attend a normal school in a normal way. He had been receiving lessons two or three times a week from a home tutor. She, Leonard and Hazel, and Mr. Hicks, Terry's prospective headmaster, all decided that it would be a sensible notion to allow Terry to go to the school a few times before he began school proper after the Christmas holidays. After their initial surprise, the schoolchildren accepted Terry as one of themselves, and Leonard and Hazel could justifiably congratulate one another on having fought and won the long battle to get the boy into a normal school. But there was yet another setback.

Just before the autumn term ended, when Terry had proved to everyone's satisfaction that he would do well at Brampton, there arrived a directive from the Ministry of Education offices in Curzon Street. It stated, without preamble, that Terry would be able to go to school in the manner agreed solely on condition that he wear his artificial arms and legs the whole time he was within the school buildings. Leonard exploded with anger, and began to write a furious reply to the Ministry. Hazel carefully restrained him. It was fortunate she did so. That evening, Mr. Hicks, Headmaster of the school, came round to the cottage. He, too, had received similar instructions from Curzon Street, and was apprehensive about what might happen if Terry were to wear his arms and legs at school.

Leonard and Hazel pointed out how ridiculous and unimaginative the directive was. Terry, stuck in the harness, could move at roughly one foot a minute; he was terrified of being knocked over in the harness, and the school was naturally full of exuberant children who some time or other must bump into the boy. If he fell there would be no protection for his head and face, and Terry would suffer extensive brain damage, blindness or death if he fell just once.

Mr. Hicks accepted their point. He wanted Terry at his school. In the boy's few visits he had captivated staff and pupils alike by his readiness to learn and his well-developed sense of mischief. Nevertheless, the Headmaster was officially a servant of the Ministry of Education: could he deliberately ignore a clear policy of theirs? Hazel and Leonard decided to play their last card. They fetched the artificial limbs and harness and, to Terry's dismay, strapped them on him in front of Mr. Hicks.

'Now walk, Terry. Walk to Mr. Hicks.'

Scared and apprehensive, Terry tried to do so. His strain and fear were apparent after only a few minute movements had been made.

'Put them away,' said Mr. Hicks. 'The boy is coming to my school, and I don't want to see him in that absurd contraption.'

That autumn of 1971 was their bleakest time. Leonard continued his struggle to bring Supercar back into existence and to rebuild all that had been lost. The new owners of the Nurseries were kind to Leonard – he was driving for them, he had been lent a one-roomed cottage as a workshop, and he had been promised that he and his family could remain at the tied cottage until they found a council bungalow – but he had to start again, borrowing, scraping, adapting whatever he could to fit his purpose. There was not one minute of any day when Leonard was unaffected by the appalling financial pressures that his struggle inflicted on the household. And for Hazel, necessarily isolated from Leonard while he was working, the anguish was even greater. Only the promise of Supercar and what it would do for Terry sustained them. The pattern of their lives had assumed the grinding monotony of extreme poverty. To fulfil even the smallest need, a cup of tea, a fire, a meal, required a great effort.

One day in November – it does not matter which; they were

all the same – gives the flavour of hard times at Nursery Cottages during that winter of 1971.

Mist lay thick along the river and its tributary streams. Still dark, and cold and damp. Leonard, having crawled into bed at two, chilled and exhausted, craving sleep with an intensity that only the truly over-extended in mind and body can know, lay utterly still like a man in a coma. The alarm clock stammered its warning. Hazel stirred, shifted, and felt the air cold on her face. Somewhere, she realized a clock was battering at her. Groaning, she propped herself on one elbow, peered for her glasses, and tugged the string that operated the overhead light. She focused on the clock. 4.30 a.m. She shuddered and turned to look at Leonard. His face, ashen, gave her cause for indecision. If she woke him now she would be denying him the sleep his constitution demanded. If she failed to wake him she would have to face his reproaches later that morning. She shook him, at first gently, then with an animation that betrayed her mounting exasperation. Not with Leonard, not with Terry, but with the whole hideous and barbaric structure of their lives. Leonard floundered into consciousness, eyes still glazed.

'It's half past four, Len.'

He grunted, and swung himself out of bed.

'My God, it's perishing in here!'

He drew on shirt, trousers and shabby sweater, then felt around for his socks. Mis-mated in black and dark blue, both had holes in the toes. Blinking, Leonard pulled them on, and found a pair of grotesquely-worn slippers. He stood, forcing himself to keep his eyes open long enough to make it downstairs to the kitchen. He paused at the door.

'Want a cup of tea, love?'

Hazel was asleep. Leonard switched off the light, and made for the kitchen.

Sheba was there to welcome him, tail thumping, eyes bright. Leonard patted her uncertainly, and tottered towards the draining-board, found last night's mug, rinsed it, and lit the gas-stove. He reached for his packet of cigarettes. Two inhalations and he was coughing briskly. The kettle boiled, and Leonard made his tea, hot, sweet and weak.

He warmed his hands round the mug and drank slowly. He was beginning to revive. Setting down his smouldering cigarette he turned on the cold tap and dashed water over his face, gasped, and towelled off. Then he left the cottage and walked past Len Curry's home towards the bothy, his new workshop.

It was still dark, and Leonard switched on the light that he had run from the kitchen to the bothy. Inside, the air was dank, and smelled of wet earth and paint and metal. Fragments of the Supercar stood about, cluttering crude benches and crates. Leonard lit another cigarette and began to examine his work on the micro-switches. He did not notice dawn staining the sky, or the irritable bickering of morning sparrows. He was planning a circuit, and it was proving tricky.

At half past seven a pale Hazel arrived at the bothy, bringing him a mug of tea and hunting for a cigarette. Leonard gave her the last one, and reluctantly left the workshop. In the kitchen there was more tea, some bread, margarine, and meat paste left by one of Hazel's friends a couple of days before. Leonard and Hazel, hunched in thought and cold, said little to one another until Leonard was about to leave for work.

'Where you off to today?'

'Hunstanton and King's Lynn.'

'Be careful, Len. You know what this mist's like.' He nodded, and kissed her.

'Bye, love.'

'Bye. Get back soon as you can.'

'I will.'

'Oh and Len – have you got a couple of bob? I shall have to go to Huntingdon today – about work.'

Leonard gave her twenty pence, which left him less than fifty to last the rest of the week.

As always, the place seemed desolate without Leonard's presence. Hazel woke Terry, washed and dressed him, and made him some toast. The calor gas ran out. One piece of bread was toasted on one side only. Terry joked about it. Hazel was less amused.

At twenty minutes to nine Hazel put Terry in the wheelchair and pushed him towards the school. The mist still lingered and her shoes rang on the metalled road. Terry chattered away, and Hazel responded as cheerfully as she could. They reached the school shortly before nine, and a teacher assumed responsibility for Terry. Hazel kissed him.

'Bye, darling. See you after school!'

'Bye, Mum. Go careful!'

Hazel walked off to the bus-stop. Two men in front of her were smoking. The sharp reassuring flavour of burning tobacco assailed Hazel with almost physical force. There would be no more cigarettes till Friday – payday – and that was two days off. The bus arrived and the waiting customers went aboard. It was ten past nine.

The clerk at the Employment Exchange was sympathetic, but unable to help. Work was scarce, and what work there was had to go first to the sole breadwinner – the man of the family. 'And, Mrs. Wiles, we don't get many requests for lady lorry-drivers, or temporary drivers, or part-time drivers of any kind.' But if Mrs. Wiles fancied a bit of cleaning? Where? He gave her an address in the town. Hazel asked around and found the avenue. Sunshine was by now perceptible, but in the quiet avenue the leaves still dripped morosely. Hazel looked at the cars parked outside the neat, solidly built semi-detached houses, at the precisely trimmed privet hedges, the well-tended gardens. A pretty woman came out of one of the houses – slim, in her twenties, smartly dressed, hair recently cut. She pushed a gleaming perambulator. Hazel paused as the young woman reached the pavement. The child was rosy, beaming, equipped with two eyes, two arms and, as far as Hazel could see, two legs. As the young woman went by Hazel caught a faint whiff of perfume.

She found the house mentioned by the clerk. The advertiser was sorry, but the job had already gone to a lady in Huntingdon. The advertiser regretted that she had failed to notify the Employment Exchange. Perhaps Hazel would kindly do so when she returned?

Light rain began to fall. Hazel's shoes were letting in water. By the time she reached the small general store her feet were wet and slippery.

'Hello, Mrs. Wiles.'

'Hello, dear.'

Hazel squeaked across to the counter.

'We're in a bit of trouble, love. Calor gas has run out, and Len doesn't get paid till Friday. D'you think you could . . .' She saw sympathy and doubt in the girl's eyes.

'I'm sorry, Mrs. Wiles. Boss said no more credit till you pay something off the bill.'

A woman entered the shop, and approached the counter. Mortified, Hazel lowered her voice.

'But what am I going to do about meals? Len'll come in Friday.'

'I'll have a word with the boss, dear. Just a minute. Yes, Mrs. Hagan, is there anything?'

Mrs. Hagan was served. Hazel waited. The assistant went off to a small room behind the shop. Hazel felt the knot in her stomach swelling. The owner came out, and beckoned Hazel over to a quiet corner of the shop, spoke to her in a low voice.

'I know how it is, Mrs. Wiles, really I do. But I've got people to pay, as well . . . and your bill's running at over thirty pounds.'

He saw the misery on Hazel's face.

'If you could just pay me . . . couple of quid?'

Hazel set down the ten pence she had left.

'That's all I've got till Friday.'

The owner was moved, embarrassed. 'I'm sorry, love. Really.'

'It's all right. Thanks anyway.'

Heavily Hazel walked out of the shop.

She was ten yards down the road when the assistant caught up with her.

'Mrs. Wiles!'

Hazel turned.

The girl was offering her a small, brown-paper-wrapped parcel. 'From the boss.'

'What? Oh. Thanks very much.'

Bewildered, Hazel watched the girl run back to the shop. The doorbell clanged. Hazel opened the little parcel: ten Player's Weights, a quarter-pound bar of chocolate, and a tin of tomato soup. Tears of gratitude and misery welled up in her eyes, blurred her spectacles.

'Oh God. Oh my God.'

Hazel reached the bus-stop. The rain was passing over. She rattled the ten pence in her coat pocket. She walked back to the cottages.

En route she stopped off at a farm. The foreman shouted a greeting. There was a quick interchange of news. Hazel took a bucket and went into the potato field. She pulled a bucketful of potatoes, and squelched back to the farmyard. She washed the mud from the potatoes, rinsed her hands and shoes, dropped the potatoes into a sack, and trudged across towards the cottage.

It was very cold inside. Hazel went to switch on the stove, then recalled that the gas had run out. The radio, she knew, lacked a battery. She took off her shoes and stockings, dried her feet, padded into the living-room, lit one of her gift cigarettes, huddled on the sofa, and looked out over the damp meadow, the sodden trees. She shuddered. She smoked the cigarette halfway down, nipped it out, and put the stub on the mantelpiece. She found a pair of Leonard's gumboots, went down to the bothy and found the axe. Then she went off across the soaking grass of the meadow towards the spinney to find kindling.

By half past twelve the cottage was unbearable, with wet, green branches sending out blue and white smoke that choked Hazel, and brought tears to her eyes. The fire would eventually catch, she knew that from experience, but it was the stage before it caught that was the trouble. Len Curry, their neighbour, home for a quick lunch, saw the smoke pouring out of the windows and ran across. He met Hazel on the path outside; she reassured him.

Stocky, quiet, amused, Len urged Hazel to have a cup of coffee at his place. There it was neat, warm, well-ordered. Len had an efficient paraffin stove. He warmed up some shepherd's pie left over from the previous evening and offered it to Hazel. She refused to share it. She knew there was enough for one only.

'What're you giving them for supper?'

'I don't know . . . stew, I think. I've got some spuds and a tin of soup . . .'

Len Curry disappeared into the kitchen and came back with a packet of barley and some Oxo cubes.

'No, Mr. Len, really . . . I can't.'

'I shan't be having stew again for ages. Go on. When I run short I'll be round at yours, don't worry!'

The afternoon stretched wet and uninviting ahead of her. Leonard would be at Hunstanton by now, she reckoned. She finished the stub-end of the cigarette and reached for the radio, then again remembered it needed new batteries. And the fire! That amount of kindling would soon be consumed. She must find something that would burn more slowly and last longer. The walk to the deserted Forest Commission area took her half an hour. Hazel found what she had been hoping for: off-cuts the men had left, fairly neatly, after felling and sawing up several old and potentially dangerous trees. She began to fill the coal-sack she had brought for the purpose. When it was too full to carry she dragged it behind her over the muddy track, and slowly back to the cottage. It was half past three. Some of the drier wood she chopped into manageable sections and put on the dwindling fire in the living-room. Then she washed her hands, changed into her damp shoes, and set off for the school and Terry.

His presence in the cottage lightened the afternoon. She toasted more bread over the smoky fire, and Terry was well pleased with the results: this was like going camping.

Leonard returned at half past seven, tired but cheerful. He had struck lucky at a transport café near King's Lynn. The woman on the day shift there had recognized Leonard from some newspaper article, and wanted to talk about Terry. As Leonard was leaving the café, homeward bound, the woman furtively gave him a plastic bag. Inside were three-quarters of a pound of bacon, an almost full bottle of Daddy's Sauce, and a Cornish pasty. Leonard had guiltily eaten the pasty in the late afternoon, but comforted himself with the knowledge that the rest of the goodies would be more than welcome. Hazel bustled, Leonard swung Terry on to his lap, and talked about the events of the day. Sheba lay by the fire, much too close, until Leonard warned her away. Hazel boiled a kettle on the living-room fire – Leonard had long ago constructed a movable hob for this purpose – then peeled the potatoes. Leonard drank his tea and went out to the bothy.

At eight he returned to have supper, a curious but filling stew of potatoes, barley, tomato soup, bacon, Daddy's Sauce and two Oxo cubes. The stale bread they had left could perfectly well be dunked in the stew. Terry's lean stomach stretched. There would be enough stew for tomorrow, and Leonard hoped to get half a dozen onions as well, from a customer he knew in St. Neots. Terry was washed and put to bed. Hazel luxuriated with another cigarette. Leonard went out to the bothy. It was now a quarter to nine.

He returned, damp and cold, close to midnight. Hazel was fast asleep on the sofa, with an old dressing-gown round her for warmth. The fire was very low, but the bricks were thoroughly heated. Leonard brought in some of the wood Hazel had collected and stacked it safely round the side of the fireplace. It would dry out overnight. He woke Hazel with a cup of tea, and urged her to go to bed.

'What about you, Len? You're exhausted. You can't keep missing sleep like this!'

'When I'm tired, I'll come to bed.'

He returned to the bothy, wearing a raincoat now for added warmth. The light went off in the bedroom. Hazel lay awake for a short while, wondering how long Leonard could continue to drive himself in this way before he cracked up. At two, Leonard realized where he had been going wrong with his system of circuitry. The knowledge that he could now see how to simplify the layout of the micro-switches acted like a cordial. Patiently he began to strip away part of the existing installation. Rummaging in his raincoat pocket he found a crumpled cigarette – bent but undamaged. He lit it, and worked on. Outside, overnight heavy traffic rumbled towards the arterial road. A fox barked once. At three in the morning a Mid-Anglia police car chased a shop-breaker at ninety miles an hour along the main road beyond the cottages. Its siren wailed and its brakes screamed. Leonard heard nothing. He had fallen asleep with his head on the bench, amongst woodshavings and iron filings, small tins of paint and two buckled sheets of glasspaper.

The long, hard summer had declined into a sour autumn and a bleak winter. There had been successes:

24th November, 1971: Terry has gone to school today, our boy was so happy when he came home, everybody was so pleased with him.

But there had been savage reversals, too: the worry over Leonard's job and the probable loss of the cottage; the constant dance with bankruptcy; the destruction of the workshop. Leonard was now sixty. His damaged back gave him pain, and he worried that he would be unable to go on driving. His obsession with the Supercar and the help it could offer Terry, however, forced him, always, back to his workshop.

CHAPTER ELEVEN

MANY INVENTIONS

To many people the life of an inventor, surrounded by the creations of his dreams, seems glamorous. The reality is more often the reverse – lonely, boring, demanding and never without frustrations. But the most heart-breaking setback occasionally leads to a release of thought, a revelation, an unexpected step towards the goal. The fire which had cremated the Bomb and the early Supercar, and had devastated Leonard's already overstretched resources, gave him still more determination to succeed, a new understanding of what he had to do and an insight into the strength and weakness of what he had done.

Terry needed not merely to lift himself a few meagre inches from the ground, but to confront people at their own level, to look into their eyes, to work at table height. The disadvantage of being twenty-one inches tall was mainly the barrier of living in a world dominated by feet and legs, a world where everything and everybody had to be looked up to. But Terry did not only need to have his eyes at the right level. He needed to be able to 'stoop': to lower himself to the floor to pick up a dropped knife, to rise immediately to place it on the table, or higher still to reach a shelf or paint a door frame. And he had to do it as quickly and as effortlessly as a normal person might. Leonard wanted to create a mechanical extension of Terry's tiny frame which simply lifted him to wherever he wanted to be as quickly and easily as possible.

The Bomb had incorporated the car jack principle, safe and easy to build, but, as anyone who has mended a puncture knows, very slow. Supercar Mark I would need something better than that. Leonard looked at the hydraulic jack used in garages to whisk cars effortlessly off their wheels. It was fast enough, but expensive, difficult to control and might leak oil on the carpets. That was not for Supercar, he decided. No, the answer was a fork-lift truck, that industrial maid-of-all-work, designed to lift crates, bales or barrels like a tame Goliath and to stack them as neatly and delicately as can be. He looked at the construction of the machine. He struggled to adapt the principle to lift and protect a tiny human load and finally found an elegant solution, built from a bicycle chain, powered by a pair of windscreen motors, and fitted with a comfortable bucket seat for Terry.

The weather was now so cold that Leonard was obliged to work in the kitchen with his sprockets and chains. Eventually the lift was complete. It would raise Terry to the level of the kitchen table in under five seconds. Now he needed a truck or trolley to carry the lift about. It had to be manoeuvrable enough to drive round the furniture in an ordinary room. It had to be slender enough to pass through ordinary doors, and stable enough not to be in danger of toppling over even with the lift as high as it would go. The Bomb, with its castors at the back and big wheels in front, had been good, but not good enough. Leonard argued that Terry must not be condemned to live indoors. He had seen the bright eye light up with excitement on fishing expeditions. Terry loved outdoor life; he enjoyed the country lanes, the flat water-meadows beside the sluggish Ouse. Supercar must be capable of going outside, of bumping up and down kerbs without risk of capsizing, of exploring hedgerows and meadows without becoming bogged down, or of hurrying him to school when he was late. And yet it must retain its good manners in the house and classroom.

Leonard built his dream car in his mind. His talent was deeper and more subtle than mere engineering skill. He did not see the problem as simply one of wheel-chair design, but as the reinterpretation of the needs of a handicapped child. He knew instinctively how those needs could be translated through an aluminium frame, metal wheels, and electric motors with their control circuits. The secret lay in understanding what needed to be done, how to build a machine that was to Terry what his arms and legs might have been, a machine which he could dominate, and whose chains and belts would respond to his brain with the sensitivity of nerves and muscles.

The vision of the mobility which Supercar could bring prompted Leonard to prepare Terry for a more active life. Terry was interested in nature and fascinated by wild-life. Leonard decided he should have a telescope and somehow managed to save enough to buy one. But how was an armless small boy to steady and focus it? Leonard took time off from Supercar. It was a kind of recreation for him to think about different problems. He mounted the telesope on a stand and made a handle to fit Terry's chin which he could use to direct the telescope. Then he fitted a small electric motor to work the focus knob, controlled by two micro-switches which Terry could reach with his flipper. When he was satisfied it worked, Leonard took Terry into the fields one Saturday morning to test it. He pointed out a rabbit sitting quite still about half a mile away. Terry lined up the telescope with his chin and adjusted the focus with his toes. Suddenly the image became clear. Terry was silent, his face strained with concentration.

'What can you see, Terry?'

'Hush, Daddy,' whispered Terry. 'If you talk he'll hear you and run away!'

It was a success, a high point in yet another trough. For Leonard, never one for compromise, had had reluctantly to accept one. His dream car, he calculated, would cost £2,000 to develop and build. Where was a man already heavily in debt to find so much money? He decided, sadly, that the dream must wait and that he would build his new lift into Supercar Mark II, using a chassis similar to that of the first prototype and therefore only suitable for indoor use. Leonard accepted the inevitable and returned to his regime of continuous work.

In January 1972, the four winter months of self-denial were rewarded: Leonard was able to bring the Supercar into the cottage for its first major test in the living-room. Apart from a final coat of paint, here it was – ready. Terry and Hazel had unbounded faith in Leonard's skill, but there always had to be the first moments of dry-mouthed expectancy. There the machine stood, tall and incongruous in the living room. Leonard and Hazel pushed the sofa and armchairs back against the walls, leaving Terry a clear area in which to manoeuvre.

'Now we sit down,' Leonard told Hazel, 'and let Terry do the work.'

'I can start now, Daddy?'

Leonard nodded. Terry slid on to the seat, which lay at ground level.

'Now the safety-belt: you know what to do.' Using his teeth and shoulder, Terry strung over the safety-belt. He was still looking up at them.

'Away you go.'

Grinning nervously, Terry leaned against the vertical control with his shoulder. Smoothly the seat moved up and up. The floorboards fell away from Terry, and the toys he had left to one side. Suddenly he was afraid.

'Keep going. You won't fall off the top.' Heart thudding, Terry maintained the pressure, and the chair continued to rise. He was now on a level with his parents' eyes . . . he was going higher still. He was above Hazel's head! The seat came to rest. There was a moment's silence. Hazel and Leonard looked up at him, Hazel in wonderment, and Leonard with pride.

'Go to the table.'

The agile toes tightened on the tiny control column. Supercar began to rotate, then move forwards, smoothly, towards the table. Terry's feet were level with the table-top. He turned to look at them, face alight:

'I don't need help any more! I can get here myself and I can feed myself!'

Abruptly he reversed the chair and moved round towards Leonard. As he advanced he was simultaneously lowering the seat until it was level with Leonard's knees. The child released the safety-belt and struggled towards his father. Leonard swung the boy on to his lap and held him tight, so that Terry could not see the tears in his eyes.

'No more legs!' Terry was yelling. 'No more chair legs and table legs and people's legs! I can start to live just like any other boy!'

Leonard only fully recognized how much he had already

achieved when Terry, at bench height, was watching his father work on some new gadget. Leonard dropped a spanner and slowly stooped to pick it up. But Terry had forestalled him. He had lowered the lift to the ground, picked up the spanner between his toes, and was on his way back up to the bench before Leonard was aware what he was doing. That evening, in the cottage, they began to discover the range of activities now open to Terry.

He could help his mother to clear or lay the table. He could play cards at normal level. He could go to the television set, select his own channel, and switch it on. He could drive into the bathroom and wash his face. He could drive into the bedroom, lower the seat slightly, and scuttle on to the bed – and in the mornings he need no longer wait for Leonard or Hazel to get him up. He could open drawers, select books from shelves.

On 8th June Leonard and Hazel took the Supercar to school, to see what help it might be there. Terry was able to use it throughout the school, and at his lessons. When he wished to go outside, he simply drove up to the Everest-Jennings powered wheel-chair, lowered his own seat to meet that of the wheel-chair, and shifted himself across to it, then drove outside to the playground to join in with the other children. Mr. Hicks and his staff, already staunch advocates of Leonard's policies, were delighted with the versatility of the Supercar, and immediately allowed Terry to use it at school as much as he wanted.

With the success of Supercar Mark I, Leonard was ready to show the world his inventions in the hope that someone would find a way to manufacture them on a wider scale. Three engineers from the Department of Health paid a visit to Nursery Cottages. He heard no more. Then the Department of Engineering at Queen Mary College, London, asked Leonard to come to them with Supercar. They studied it for two weeks. He was paid £400 for his idea and any future developments. The chair, which Queen Mary College eventually produced, however, apart from the underlying concept of the lift, bore almost no relation to Supercar. 'Meteor', as their version was called, had a wide, filled-in base which could not ride over a step and it took two minutes instead of Supercar's five seconds to rise from the ground to full height. Leonard was not impressed. The

College have since released Leonard from his contract with them and he is no longer associated with their chair.

This experience with Queen Mary College made Leonard's stubborn loner's mind even more convinced that the people to help the handicapped were not engineers with degrees, or university research departments, but amateurs like himself who had to live with the problems every hour of the day and night.

So Leonard set about drawing his plans for the indoor/outdoor chair which would give Terry the freedom he really needed and waited for enough money to implement them. In the meantime, he again set his mind to other things that an eager, determined little boy could do. Terry liked animals. Could he ride a horse? But without legs how could he stay in the saddle? And without arms how was he to control the reins? Leonard remembered the discarded tin legs with their leather bucket top into which Terry's torso fitted. If he could find a flat-topped saddle, like the ones Romanies used, perhaps he could fit the bucket to it to form a saddle from which Terry could not be thrown. Word about his scheme got around, and someone found and gave him exactly the type of saddle he was looking for. The local riding school donated the services of Freddie, a docile pony on which Terry took his first ride. In prospect it all seemed marvellous. Terry the cowboy. Terry the show jumper, the champion jockey. The fantasies rushed through his head. But when he was lifted into the saddle, so high above the ground that even Leonard had to reach up to him, he felt frightened and insecure. But it did not take long: lumbering Freddie, docile and dependable, gradually overcame his fears.

Soon Leonard was at work with grand plans to enable Terry to control the horse himself instead of having to be led. He attached outriggers to the saddle, and gave Terry a little harness to which the reins were fixed, so that by leaning one way or the other, he could turn the horse to right or left, or stop it. The horse was now entirely under his control. Hazel was given a little hacking jacket for him, from which she removed the arms, and Leonard arranged that the reins could be clipped to Terry's harness inside the armholes. That day Leonard and Hazel watched with pride as Terry and Freddie cautiously rode around the paddock unaided. 'Yippee!' was Terry's only comment.

But Leonard wanted Terry to realize that he could do useful work, as well as amusing himself. Secretly, without telling Hazel, he decided he would teach the boy to saw wood on an old bandsaw in the workshop. He built a gadget to fit over Terry's shoulders with which he could guide the wood into the saw. He explained it to Terry.

'Mummy needs some firewood,' said Leonard. 'Here's a block of wood. Get cracking.'

Terry sat on the bench with the gadget fixed to his shoulders. Within seconds he was sawing away confidently, and singing at the top of his voice. When the kindling was ready he turned to Leonard with a mischievous glint in his eyes.

'There's one thing I can't do,' he said.

'Oh yes. What's that?'

'Cut my fingers off!'

And the armless boy shrieked with laughter, in which Leonard joined. Both he and Hazel had been delighted to see that, as the memory of Chailey and his handicapped friends became fainter, Terry was able to laugh at his own deformities, without self-pity or anger.

Terry got on to Supercar, collected the kindling, and drove off to the cottage whooping loudly. Hazel was at first unable to believe he had managed the sawing himself; but she was by now beginning to realize that Terry and Leonard refused to write off anything as impossible.

In September of that year Terry was able to make use of Leonard's fishing aids (which he had managed to improve greatly) in competition. A Junior Angling Contest was held, and there were some thirty enthusiastic young contenders, amongst them Terry.

> *2nd September, 1972:* Terry fished his first fishing match he won Third Prize got a medal as well We are so proud of him.

Terry was finding his feet and the Wileses were encouraged.

But within a fortnight Leonard came home, pale and stiff with pain. His back was again troubling him.

With Leonard temporarily bedridden, Hazel continued working with Terry in her own way. She determined to improve the agility of his left flipper, with its prehensile toes. She encouraged him to spend as much time as possible in exercising the toes, in using them to write smaller characters and more neatly, and to draw and paint with them. As Leonard's inventions had improved, so Terry spent more time sitting on his bottom, and Hazel was anxious that he should have as much exercise as possible when he was not in Supercar or his wheelchair. She encouraged him to strengthen his stomach muscles by finding new ways to sit upright from a lying position. Eventually, when Leonard fixed a tiny ramp on the floor, Terry was able to wriggle on to this, and by regular rocking and flexing of his stomach muscles, he was able to sit upright.

One activity only seemed likely to defeat him – going up and down stairs. Together, Hazel and Terry conquered the problem. By experiment, Hazel showed Terry that if he did slip on one tread, his buttocks and flippers could fairly readily secure him on the next one down. When Leonard was out they began more daring experiments, until Terry was able to haul himself up six or seven treads without fear.

Hazel was preparing supper one day when she heard a shout:

'Mummy! Come quickly!'

Her old fears returned. Had the dog turned on the child? She moved quickly into the living-room. Sheba was on the floor, alone and half asleep. She looked up at Hazel and yawned.

'Mummy! Here!'

Terry's voice was coming from the staircase. Hazel walked through. Terry was at the top of the stairs, grinning down at her. For a moment Hazel was tempted to shout, 'Just stay there, quite still, and I'll come and get you.'

But she realized immediately that the boy had achieved a miracle. A twenty-one-inch child without arms had climbed a fourteen-foot staircase.

'All right,' she said. 'Now let's see you come down again.'

Terry mimicked a fanfare of trumpets and began sliding and

bumping down. Once or twice Hazel almost ran to his help, but she knew now that Terry had confidence. He skidded down to the foot of the stairs and lay grinning up at her.

'How was that?'

'Come on. You can have a biscuit.'

Her work with Terry had bred in Hazel an increasing interest in helping other children. She became assistant to a Cub-mistress in a nearby village and, after attending for a few weeks, she asked her friend if Terry could come along – to watch. The Cub-mistress readily agreed. Terry went along – to watch. Within a few minutes he was scrimmaging around on the floor with the other boys in a violent game of 'British Bulldog'.

'He'd better join, Hazel, hadn't he?'

Before long, Hazel became an Akela in her own right, and had the satisfaction of seeing Terry become a fully-fledged Cub Scout. He was soon anxious to start passing proficiency tests. Hazel drew the line at examining him herself, and her friend said she was well satisfied with Terry's abilities. Hazel had privately wondered how Terry would manage with the various knots required of any self-respecting Cub, but Terry's now nimble toes found methods of dealing with them all, and soon he was instructing awed beginners into the mysteries of sheep-shank and reef-knot.

With Leonard and Terry, Hazel never ceased to be encouraging and hopeful. Her fears she confided only to her diary. While Leonard realized she was keeping one, he had no idea whatsoever of its contents. It was only years later, when the need for a silent confidant had passed, that he looked at her record of these early years of tension and disappointments and small, vital steps forward. In the autumn of that year, when Leonard was resolutely overspending to advance the new Supercar, Hazel wrote a long and poignant note:

> *9th October, 1972:* It seems to me that Len will not be working at the Garden Centre much longer I do not know what will happen then. I have said this so many times, we take two steps forward an three back I cannott see us getting on no matter what we try to do. I have no Idea what Len will do it gets me down at times I dont see how we can go

into a new house we have nothing to take into it, our bed is no good we need blankets sheets and pillows.

I would like these things for our new home but I dont suppose I shall ever get them. Dinner Service, Curtains, Pillows, Double Bed, Blanckets, Sheets, Cutlery, Tea & Coffee Service, Washing Machine, Bathroom set, Cooker, 3-piece Suite, Carpets, Standard Lamp, Dining Room Suite.

I cant see us getting a nice home Len says it will be a long time before we get anything from Distillers if we get anything at all.

Hazel realized that for Supercar and their future a miracle was needed. It happened, quite unexpectedly, in a telephone call from the *Sunday Times*.

14th November, 1972: Marjorie from the Sunday Times came today shes very nice she wants to come again its very foggy.

This short note in Hazel's diary masks the anxiety she and Leonard felt about the visit. They had known many offers of help before, and had watched enthusiasm and interest peter out. They had read with mixed feelings other articles about thalidomide and had no idea what to expect. Their hopes had been raised and dashed many times over the years. But they had always felt that publicity would help to create a bond of sympathy and understanding between the able-bodied and the handicapped. The interview lasted for several hours and was followed by a second visit two days later, with Marjorie's colleague, Phillip Knightley. Leonard thought that their story would run perhaps to as much as half a column, and went down to the village on Sunday morning to buy the paper. 'To say I was astonished is an understatement,' he wrote. 'I had recognized in Marjorie sensitivity and determination. But I had not expected a whole page, beautifully put, getting across what we had achieved and our hopes for the future.' Later, when he was able to see how the article was going to affect their lives, he wrote: 'I was overwhelmed with the generosity of ordinary people. . . . I knew that what I had done, and was going to do, could help so many along the road to the freedom that Terry had achieved, and it was impossible to do it alone. . . .'

The Wileses' lives changed dramatically within a few days of publication of the article on 19th November.

21st November, 1972: We have had quite a few nice letters from the S.T. Readers with money . . . it is wonderfull.

23rd November, 1972: Terry got a parcel from the BBC today. We got £35 in letters . . . Len has now got really going on Supercar.

By the time Hazel was writing this last entry, over £200 had arrived at the cottage for the family, and Hazel jubilantly recorded:

1st December, 1972: A letter from Jack Ashley, M.P. I find it all rather overwhelming.

12th December, 1972: We have been invited to the House of Commons, Terry got a parcel of books £10 also came in the post.

18th December, 1972: I have now got a lovely home Im no longer ashamed of it got the tree done and all the trimmings and I am sure we are going to be able to give Terry a wonderfull Xmas . . . the coal shed is full and so is the Pantry.

Christmas Day, 1972: The best Xmas we have ever had, Terry had lots of things Len got me a Radio Terry bought me a Table lighter. A great day gosh im tired

By the New Year they had received donations amounting to £2,000. When Leonard and Hazel had replied to every signed letter and gift, the time had come for Leonard to think again about the dream car. He needed a proper workshop, and eventually bought for £50 a 27-foot caravan, which the local police, always helpful, delivered to the cottage. Len stripped much of the inside and turned it into a makeshift workshop. Immediate freedom from financial worry enabled him to work with greater enthusiasm than ever. He knew now that Hazel, with a comfortable home round her, would be less lonely.

One year after the *Sunday Times* article had appeared, Supercar Mark II was complete. It had all the advantages of the previous Supercars, and many more. The seat could still lift Terry six feet high, but now it could also bound over rough fields and climb kerbs.

The October morning was mild, the sun gradually dispersing the low-lying mists. Blackbirds chackered, and overhead a jet thundered. Outside the cottage stood Supercar Mark II, looking like a tall throne. The tiny child looked up at it.

'Can I go now?'

'Hop in.'

Terry eased on to the lift seat, fixed his safety belt, then raised himself to three feet above the ground. Hazel put a small basket by his side.

'All right,' she said. 'Go and pick me some blackberries.'

Terry's toes moved forwards to the control. Noiselessly Supercar spun round through ninety degrees. The child was hidden behind the high upright of the vehicle.

'See you!' he called, and the machine moved forwards. Leonard tensed a little – would Supercar climb the grass verge with Terry aboard? Supercar did, taking the sharpish incline like an educated tank. Then it sped forwards over the squeaking weeds and into the meadow, leaving black wheeltracks on the wet grass.

Terry was alone and crossing open country. He was a corporal in a jeep: he was a Crusader on a horse: he was a Tank Commander in the desert. He was a boy, bounding and heaving over uneven meadows towards a long, inviting hedge filled with plump blackberries. Terry began to sing in a high, pure alto. He was a boy looking for blackberries, and he could do it as well as any of his pals at school. Better! He flicked the controls and zoomed up four, five, six feet. He was looking down at the low hedge. *He* was looking *down* at something! Twenty-one inches high and he could see over the hedge to the meadow beyond, where a quiet mare swished her tail and dreamed in the early morning sunlight. Terry swung the machine alongside the hedge, chose his bunch of blackberries, and his small brown toes reached forward to grasp it. They could hear him singing a quarter of a mile away. Arm in arm, standing by the front door of the cottage, Leonard and Hazel were content for Terry to have his morning of wonder uninterrupted.

'My God, Len,' Hazel said after a while. 'You've really done it this time!'

He squeezed her hand, and said nothing. There was nothing he wanted to say.

An hour later Terry reappeared, a small grinning boy hooting at them across the meadow. He bumped over uneven ground and guided Supercar over the last grass verge, on to the lane by the cottage. His bright brown eye was full of laughter, and there were purple stains round his mouth.

'Terry, where are the blackberries you were supposed to be picking for me?'

Terry assumed a sombre expression, then howled with laughter.

'Tarumtara!' he declaimed, and assumed an atrocious American accent. 'Police today are searching for Terrence Wiles, in connection with a recent robbery. Wiles, eleven years old, is almost two foot high, has no arms and no legs, and was last seen driving a green Supercar along the Brampton bypass. He is known to be dangerous, and has recently eaten two pounds of blackberries.'

PART THREE

The Way We Live Now

CHAPTER TWELVE

A MAN OF VISION

On 21st March, 1974, the day the Wiles family moved into a specially designed council bungalow, Hazel's diary came to an end. She no longer felt the need to chronicle in her round handwriting and unpunctuated phrases all the deprivations she dared not reveal elsewhere. After two *Sunday Times* articles, one in the autumn of 1972 and one in the spring of the following year, their lives had changed. For the first time since they were married they did not have to plead with bailiffs or scuffle with debts. Hazel could drive into Huntingdon and choose a carpet or a three-piece suite or look at a washing machine. She could enjoy suburban luxuries unimagined in her caravan childhood and tormented adolescence.

They also received their first instalment of the compensation offered by Distillers Biochemicals, the British manufacturers of thalidomide, and as adoptive parents and guardians they were entitled to £5,000 for their own use. This soon disappeared, for Leonard still had an overdraft of £3,000. Most of the money, as usual, had been spent on materials and tools. This was the one area in which Leonard refused to stint. Cautious in every other way, he was relentless in his waste when it came to any possible improvement to the design of Terry's chair. In a style more suited to the chief designer of a Rolls-Royce engine than a self-employed amateur, he would discard sheet after expensive sheet of aluminium until the proportions of the chair were matched exactly to the child's needs and the potential of the machine. At odd moments in the early morning or during a sleepless hour in the night, Leonard could be seen standing in front of his invention. Like a fisherman who has netted a mermaid, he would gaze with awe at the creature his handiwork had captured and his mind would drift into extravagant dreams.

But Leonard was not a man to be content with dreams. During the summer of 1974 he completed Supercar Mark III, the best of them all, the car which Terry now uses. He had sacrificed some of the flamboyant features of Mark II, such as its ability to climb high kerbs and ride rough ground, for more subtle performance in the house or on the road. Most important, he had succeeded in reducing the overall size of Supercar, making it one of the most elegant yet powerful machines ever intended for a handicapped young man. With two inches tapered from the seat, it could pass through the narrowest cottage door, spin round on its own axis in a three-foot space and yet remain every bit as stable as the plumper Mark II – so stable in fact that it could take the 23-stone combined weight of Leonard and another man standing on the back, drive at 4 m.p.h. and turn a sharp bend without toppling its passengers or showing any signs of strain. 'It's like a London bus,' says Leonard, 'you can tilt it to 45 degrees before it falls over.' In addition, Leonard accepted Cambridge Consultants' offer to build a new electronic system with even more exact controls, which more than halved the power needed so that Supercar Mark III could work all day without running the batteries down. Not every family, Leonard realized, had the time to adapt their homes, constantly re-charge batteries and devote themselves to one child. Supercar would have to be tough, reliable and move safely in the most cluttered rooms.

For Leonard's ambitions did not stop with Terry. Already he could see in Supercar the possibility of liberating thousands of people with missing or paralysed limbs, crippled children who would no longer have to live entangled in adult legs but could, like Terry, rise up and talk eye to eye; older people living alone, haunted by the fear of falling and being unable to reach for help. Given such a chair they could shift along the floor into the seat and raise themselves to the height of a telephone.

As his visions of adapting Supercar expanded, he planned how he might make them more practical. He even envisaged setting up a small unit based at home where he would train students from the local technical colleges. Unlike the conventional classes their course would be mainly in observation. They would learn to watch the handicapped person, to record in their minds every muscle he used – at what times and to what effect – and only at the end of weeks or maybe months would they begin their designs, shaping the devices, like a dressmaker, around the disabled person's needs.

Leonard, however, still held on to his sense of healthy realism. His experience of the blunt imaginations of some civil servants and the caution of those who influence government decisions had persuaded him that any chair or aid had first to conform with official requirements regardless of its use for the handicapped person. Tired of forcing his visions on half-blind eyes, he decided to give up the struggle. He spent the early months of 1974 living quietly at home on his invalid pension, developing his ideas. He no longer sought the attention of the outside world. He waited for it to come to him.

He did not wait long. One afternoon in late summer, when he was busy in the workshop and Hazel lay asleep on her cherished sofa, a British Rail van pulled up in the road outside their house and a pale young Irishman jumped out. Hazel answered the door.

'Hello!' said the Irishman. 'Are you the Wileses with the little thalidomide boy whose picture was in the paper?' Hazel nodded.

'I've been trying to find out where you lived for ages and then back at the station they gave me this parcel to deliver. It's the luck of the devil. Can I come in and have a word?'

The door closed. Four hours later, as the sun went down, the British Rail van was still parked outside the Wileses' front door.

CHAPTER THIRTEEN

GORDON AND TRACEY

GORDON O'CONNOR and his family came to live in Huntingdon several years ago. Their two sons were normal, active boys but Tracey, their twelve-year-old daughter, was severely damaged by spina bifida. Both her legs were paralysed, she was incontinent, and her tiny spine was so twisted and humped that it pushed her chest out like a pack in front of her and bent her body into a lop-sided S. But despite these deformities, Tracey was a pretty girl with a calm, sweet expression and captivating smile.

Neither Gordon nor his wife had experience of physical handicap before Tracey was born. Through the early years she underwent operation after operation until she was covered in scars but the surgery was unsuccessful and the doctors announced she would never walk. The O'Connors had to face a future of lifting her in and out of her canvas wheel-chair and adjusting to life with a dependent cripple. But they were not the kind of family to accept helplessness when anything more positive could be tried. Gordon O'Connor had fought the education authorities and succeeded in removing Tracey from a special school and placing her in the local primary school. There, Tracey's gentleness and courage soon dispelled any anxieties and she and her wheel-chair became popular features in the school. Gordon was not content. The trouble, he realized, was that she lived her life on one plane – at the level of the wheel-chair – so that to achieve anything at all she needed someone constantly by her side. Like Leonard, he had diagnosed the problem, but, unlike Leonard, he had no engineering skill to help him find a solution.

'Len!' shouted Hazel above the noise of the welder. 'There's an admirer here who wants to have a word with you.'

Leonard did not reply.

Gordon stood nervously behind Hazel at the door of the garage workshop. He had not expected to see so stern and powerful a figure and Leonard, when he was concentrating, was formidable. To anyone who had not lived with his single-minded absorption in his inventions, he could appear arrogant and off-hand.

'Len!' Hazel repeated, 'he's got a spina bifida girl. Will you come and talk to him?'

Reluctantly, Leonard acknowledged Gordon, switched off the machine and came to shake hands. During the next four hours they talked about Tracey and her problems and what Leonard might do to help. When Gordon left, his van was still full of undelivered parcels. At the next house, the woman at the door shouted after him.

'Young man! I think you've made a mistake. The parcel you brought is for Mr. and Mrs. Wiles . . .'

Gordon smiled and took the parcel. He must have held on to it all this time. It was a good excuse. Tomorrow he would go back to the Wileses' and take Tracey with him. In the meantime Leonard, impressed by the Irishman's obvious passion for his daughter and his insistence that something could be done to help, began to sketch in his mind the adaptations he would have to make to Supercar. By the time Gordon and Tracey arrived, he was already dismantling the seat of one of Terry's early chairs and fixing a flap to support the useless weight of legs.

That day marked the beginning of a lively friendship between the two families and, more important, it was the breakthrough Leonard had needed to prove that Supercar could help children other than Terry.

By the weekend he had adapted the old chair sufficiently for Tracey to try it out. The machine had no motor and only makeshift controls but the lift mechanism worked. Tracey was able to rise from the ground until she was six feet tall. It was the second time that Leonard had witnessed joy on the face of a child liberated by his own invention. His eyes filled with tears.

Seeing that such a crude adaptation worked so well, Leonard and Gordon settled down to the business of building a new Supercar.

It was no easy task. Gordon spent all his free time and much of British Rail's, working with Leonard on the improvements. In fact the van was seen so often parked outside the Wileses' house that his colleagues began to tease him.

'So, who's the little woman you're keeping down in Miller Way?' they jibed.

Gordon laughed. The only 'other woman' in his life had four small wheels and a metal frame. Weeks passed and the van was no longer to be seen. Gordon had become seriously ill and had lost his job. In some ways he did not mind. As he recovered, he could spend more and more time pottering about the workshop and thinking about his daughter's chair.

Broken blades and drills littered the floor where he had been at work. Yet Leonard never complained about his enthusiastic, ham-handed apprentice. He encouraged Gordon to design and watched patiently as the young man padded the back and distorted the proportions of the seat. He wanted Gordon to find out for himself.

The first trial was a disaster. The padding left so little room for Tracey that she hung over the edge like a bird dangling from a nest. His face fell. How could he have made so stupid a mistake? He turned away to avoid the reproach in his daughter's eyes. But there was none. Just happiness that her father had tried so hard, and confidence that he would succeed.

In July 1975, fifteen months after their first meeting, 'Pathfinder', as they called Tracey's chair, was ready. It was similar to Supercar but the seat was much more complicated, with arms which hinged down either side, and a flap for her legs which could be raised level with any surface. There Tracey sat, keeper of three drawbridges which she could let down at will and across which she could reach the outside world. By lowering the arm flaps, or raising the leg flaps, she could swing her body out in any direction.

Within a few hours Tracey had mastered the controls and after some days of running the batteries dry, negotiating obstacles on the Wileses' lawn, she was allowed to take Pathfinder home.

She soon learned to manoeuvre the machine around the house. She could get out of bed in the mornings by rolling on to the seat across one of the drawbridges. Then she would drop to the floor to fetch her shoes or rise up again to the cupboard to take down a blouse. For the first time, she could dress herself unaided. Gradually the O'Connors began to realize the revolution that was taking place in their lives. Tracey, who had always been sitting where they had last put her down, was suddenly nowhere to be seen.

She would be in the kitchen washing the dishes, or outside in the garden or searching for a gramophone record from the shelf. One day she dropped her hat. Gordon, by habit, stooped to pick it up, but was reprimanded by his daughter.

'Don't, Dad!' she said, 'I can pick it up myself,' and within seconds she had zoomed down to the floor and up again with the hat triumphantly in her hands.

Now Tracey and Terry could drive off together, Terry, the old hand, bellowing instructions and showing the way. They raced down the street in their red and orange supercars – the limbless, thalidomide boy and the spina bifida girl.

'Charge!' shouted Terry, zig-zagging like a red rag in front of her.

'I'm going to beat you if it kills me!' Tracey swung out to overtake.

Both were so skilled that their machines responded to them as if they were their own legs. They nearly collided, laughed and drove on. Terry started to sing. For a moment, as their parents watched them disappearing around the corner, they forgot their tiny, deformed bodies – they were just two normal, happy children running out to play.

CHAPTER FOURTEEN

A WAY TO INDEPENDENCE

AT the age of twelve, Terry became a wealthy young man. After eleven years of legal wrangling and bitter disputes, Distillers Biochemicals, while still denying negligence, had offered the thalidomide children generous compensation. Following an intensive press, public and parliamentary campaign, they had, during the course of 1972–73 increased this offer from £3¼ million to more than £26 million. By July 1973 nearly every parent had accepted and the long and unhappy battle was won. The money was to be shared out among the 400 victims according to the severity of their damage, partly in the form of private trusts and partly as a Thalidomide Children's Trust to which all the children could apply. Terry was assessed by a panel of doctors and awarded the maximum damages. A year later, in the summer of 1974, the first payments arrived.

The money did not, of course, go straight into Terry's hands. His trust was strictly administered by trustees, including his adoptive parents, and it was handed out only for Terry's specific personal needs.

One of the first of these was to buy a bungalow in his own name which could be adapted permanently and where, if necessary, he could spend the rest of his life. It was Terry who chose the house. Since the spring term, he had been going to Ernulf's Comprehensive School at St. Neots, ten miles south of Brampton, and Leonard and Hazel were exhausted by the distance they had to drive each day. Then one day, by chance, they came across an advertisement for a house within easy distance of the school. Terry took one look at the garden at the back, the large living room and all the places where he could park his chair without being in the way and whooped with delight.

'This is it, Mum,' he whispered to Hazel. 'And it's got an open fire-place too.'

Impatient as ever with official dilly-dallying, the Wiles family did not wait for the contracts to be exchanged. A week before Christmas, they packed the van with suitcases and moved in.

'With a child like Terry,' Leonard often said, 'time is of the essence.' He knew that Terry's race to self-sufficiency still depended on his own health and inventiveness, and as he was 62 and suffering from diabetes, no time could be lost. As soon as they had moved in Leonard set to work to adapt the house. He fixed special levers to the front of the sink so that by using his flippers and holding the glass in his mouth, Terry could pour himself a glass of water. He improved the doors, built ramps on the steps outside and installed a Swedish toilet with jets of water and hot air. Terry was amused. As he sat for the first time to try it out, a jet of water leaped several feet into the air.

'Oooh!' he shouted to Hazel. 'Have you got a gun?'

'What on earth do you want a gun for?'

'Well, you know those ping-pong balls at the fair? I'm just like one. You'll have to shoot me down!'

With the new toilet, Terry could attend to his own needs. He could drive into the bathroom in his Supercar, adjust his chair to the height of the toilet seat and shuffle across. There was a simple but effective device for his toothbrush at the side of the sink. He could, by adjusting the seat of his chair to the level of the mattress, slide on to his tiny 'Goldilocks' bed and, by using his shoulder blade or flippers, switch on his own light, radio or television. An ingenious perspex extension to the telephone enabled him to ring up his friends. For luxury living, he could turn on a switch to operate the fountain in the pool outside his bedroom window.

Outside in the garden there was a wooden chalet with a low knob on the door. This was Terry's den. No adult was allowed to enter without permission. It was here that he entertained. For hours, he and his special friend, Tony, would play darts or pontoon. Terry had mastered the art not only of dealing with his flippers but also of gambling. It was here, too, that Terry often did his homework. Despite the large, tougher classes of the comprehensive school, he could still hold his own. He would ride to school in Supercar or drive it up into the back of his father's van and once at school, apart from the toilet, he needed little extra help. The nurse assigned by the local authority to attend to Terry often found herself with little to do.

Terry recalls his first day at his new school, frighteningly large and important. As he drove, Len walking by his side through corridors and classrooms filled with the murmurs of children at work, they came to a carpeted area and Terry was suddenly aware of somebody looking down at him.

'Terry, this is Mr. Slater, your new teacher,' said Len.

'Hello, Sir,' Terry said shyly, too overcome to lift himself in his chair.

'Come on up,' said Len.

Terry touched Supercar's controls and in a moment was on a level with his teacher.

'How did you do that?' Mr. Slater asked.

Terry explained that he worked the lift with his shoulder, and the apprehension was gone. As he was shown the school, a bell for break rang and the silent corridors were filled with bustling children looking curiously at the little figure in his extraordinary car. Before long Leonard and Mr. Slater left him in the library answering questions from a crowd of children.

'Were you born like that, mate?'

'Yes.'

'You haven't got any arms?'

'No, but it doesn't bother me.'

'Witty, ain't you? How old are you?'

'Twelve.'

'What's your name?' asked a small boy.

'Terry.'

'Come on then, Terry. Let's go for a walk.'

'Anything to get away from this mob.'

Terry started Supercar forcing his way through the crowd with his new friend Tony by his side.

That was eighteen months ago. The headmaster, who had

been reluctant to take Terry into the school, now admits he has proved himself and is accepted by the other pupils. He has even learned to turn his disabilities to his own advantage. In his machine Terry is more than a match for the toughest bully. His quick wit and well-aimed dummy charges from Supercar soon scatter opponents and have made him a popular ring-leader of the classroom gang.

In most school subjects he is average but he is extraordinarily well-read – his bookcase is lined with glossy encyclopaedias – and his ability to express himself is far advanced for his age. He has learned to type, using a Possum typewriter adapted by his father with a keyboard of eight micro-switches, but he still prefers to write with his rudimentary feet.

During the years, Leonard and Hazel had noticed that Terry always used his left flipper for writing or grasping; the right one only served to hold the paper down. It was this weakness in his right foot which prompted Leonard to teach Terry his latest hobby. With money from the Trust, he bought a radio-controlled model aircraft, a skill tricky enough to master with two normal hands and impossible for Terry unless he used both 'feet' to their full potential. Terry, thrilled by the sight of the delicate wings brushing the trees and diving and spinning through the clouds, unconsciously began to manipulate every available muscle.

'There's not much he can't do,' said Leonard with a grin. 'By the time he is in his late teens we want him to have tried everything possible. He will know that he can shoot an arrow, hurl darts, ride, sew, cook, grow vegetables or play the organ. He doesn't need to do all of them now but he can choose to go back to them when he is older. The important thing is that he attempted them when he was young: he need never feel that while I was alive any opportunity was denied.'

But all these gadgets and adaptations would be mere ornaments without Supercar. The red 'miracle' is the centre of all their lives. Without it, Terry the tall prince is changed back into a tiny frog, hopping at their feet, lifted from place to place and dependent on help for every move. The house, the garden and the van are all built around the chair and, like a splash of red in a crowded painting, it gives a focus and meaning to the whole.

Leonard is justifiably proud. Lack of interest from the outside world has not dampened his ambition. Recently he has tried Tracey's Pathfinder on a twenty-two-year-old girl, paralysed from the waist down. Despite her extra weight, she was soon driving about the house. Suddenly, like Terry and Tracey, she was released from the prison of life at one level. She could pick up papers from the floor and at seven feet; for the first time since her illness, she could hang out her own washing. It is this freedom, this expansion of life that Leonard would like to give to other handicapped people. But it is not, he feels, something that you can describe.

'Our real story,' he says, 'cannot be told in a book. A book is just words. This is a war of movement.'

EPILOGUE

Were I so tall to reach the pole,
Or grasp the ocean in my span,
I must be measured by my soul.
The mind's the standard of the man.
Isaac Watts

Just looking at a child like Terry, turns you into a kind of visionary. *Leonard Wiles*

It is now over eight years since Leonard first saw the scrap of humanity that was Terry, sitting on his bed in the ward of Chailed Heritage. In those years Terry has not grown – he is still only two feet high and weighs less than a child of two, but he has developed into an ebullient, articulate young man. He is unembarrassed by his deformities and he is afraid of nothing. At fourteen he has his future well mapped out: when he finishes school he plans to find work helping to design aids for the handicapped. For Leonard and Hazel have succeeded in toppling the tower of Terry's helplessness and making him aware of the needs of other people. Underneath his schoolboy repartee, there is an almost missionary dedication to the disabled and to the inventions which he and his adoptive father might devise to help them. By combining both their talents and his own money he feels sure they will succeed.

Terry has learned from Leonard and Hazel a developing faith in God. Like them, he is convinced that it was no mere chance which spliced their three lives together. He firmly believes that God has compensated him for his lack of arms and legs by bringing him such parents and by endowing him with so many other gifts.

He intends to marry – a normal girl. A few years ago even Leonard and Hazel tried to dissuade him from this hope, but now with his sexual organs developing as in any teenage boy, with his pride in his neat, brown body and his buoyant personality, they believe that he will succeed.

Nothing will deter Terry now. Sometimes when they sit and reflect on the years since Terry came into their lives, they have the uncomfortable suspicion that they have only been pawns in the master plan of an obstinate little boy. After all, it was he who had fastened himself on to their lives when they had no need of him and now, a healthy young man with financial, and to a certain extent physical, independence, it is he who has less need of them. In theory, when he is eighteen, he can ask them to leave his house.

But Leonard and Hazel were not the kind of people to be manipulated against their will. They had their plans too. From the first days, when Terry's disabilities dominated life at Nursery Cottages, they were determined to unshackle his pathetic little body from its limitations and set him free. Nothing was done by accident: every gadget they made and every book or toy they bought were all part of an overall scheme. Through the years, the poverty, the fire, the frustrations, the successes and failures, with extraordinary patience and imagination, they carved out Terry's future, leading him step by step towards independence. Now they feel they are not far from their goal.

Most important of all, they have taught him to accept and return their love.

MY STORY BY URI GELLER

Ever since he burst upon an astonished world a few years ago in a wave of bending spoons, stopped clocks and wilting door-keys, Uri Geller has been the centre of a storm of public and scientific controversy. Scientists have been able to find no logical explanation for the things he can do: his amazing powers of telepathy and clairvoyance have stunned the most sceptical observers . . .

Now he tells his own story – from his childhood in Israel, when 'strange things' first began to happen, to the present, when worldwide fame has made Uri Geller one of the sensations of the seventies . . .

0 552 10391 8 85p

THE LINK BY MATTHEW MANNING

WHEN HE WAS ELEVEN, MATTHEW'S HOME BECAME THE SCENE OF REPEATED ASSAULTS BY A POLTERGEIST

It was Matthew, rather than his younger brother or his sister who was thought to be the source of the disturbances. His anxious parents were advised that in a few weeks the phenomena would cease and the family could settle down to live normally again. As predicted, the poltergeist withdrew.

BUT WHEN MATTHEW WAS FIFTEEN, THE PHENOMENA RECURRED WITH FAR GREATER POWER AND VIOLENCE . . .

Matthew was by then a boarder at a public school. The events which followed were some of the most extraordinary ever recorded in psychic history. And it was Matthew himself who found a way of quelling the disturbances; by allowing himself to be used by unknown forces, he produced drawings in the style of Picasso, Aubrey Beardsley, Paul Klee, and many others, and messages from thousands of people of different nationalities, living in former times.

0 552 99955 5 75p

JUDY GARLAND BY ANNE EDWARDS

In this brilliant, deeply human and glittering book – the definitive biography of Garland the star, Judy the woman – Anne Edwards has re-created the life, the loves, the sorrows, the joys, the disasters of a legendary woman. Drawing on a wealth of previously unavailable material, on the intimate revelations of those who knew and loved Judy, on her own meeting with Judy Garland, on the memories of friends, fans, strangers and contemporaries, she has written a book that is sensational in its revelations of the truth behind the Garland legend and the Garland headlines, and at the same time hauntingly, heartbreakingly moving and compassionate; at last, the great, major book that Judy Garland's life deserved.

0 552 10063 3 75p

I, TOM HORN BY WILL HENRY

. . . I must leave this truth where it will be found. The story is all told, all written down, waiting only to be passed to the one who will get it from me tonight when he comes for the last time. No one could have told this story but me. I rode that trail in Wyoming alone. From the first day, it was Tom Horn against the pack . . .

The Old West that Tom Horn knew lived and died with him. When he was gone, the West was gone. In I, TOM HORN, Will Henry recreates the man and his times through a first-person narrative, as a possible lost autobiography of the legendary cowboy. Those who read it will always wonder . . . was this man guilty, or did his enemies kill him to make innocents of themselves?

0 552 10105 2 65p